Songs Of My Heart

Songs Of My Heart

Beshera

authorHOUSE®

AuthorHouse™
1663 Liberty Drive
Bloomington, IN 47403
www.authorhouse.com
Phone: 1-800-839-8640

First published by AuthorHouse   01/18/2015

ISBN: 978-1-4634-1027-8 (sc)
ISBN: 978-1-4634-1499-3 (e)

Library of Congress Control Number: 2011908643

Print information available on the last page.

Any people depicted in stock imagery provided by Thinkstock are models, and such images are being used for illustrative purposes only.
Certain stock imagery © Thinkstock.

This book is printed on acid-free paper.

My testimony to God,

On January 18, 2009 I sprained my ankle, I went to the doctor, and I wore a boot for about two or three weeks. On April the 12, 2009, I went into the hospital with multiple blood clots in my lungs. I was actually breathing off a partial lung. For that many blood clots to have been moving through my heart for such a long time. I was surprise that I did not have a heart attack with that many blood clots going through my heart. My ankle kept swelling that is why I had so many blood clots in my lungs. For over a month or more my breathing was extremely bad, some times it seem like I could not breathe at all. I was advised it was my weight, but apparently it wasn't. That Easter Sunday morning the pain was so bad I could not stand up strength. That's why I had to call for an ambulance it was the only alternative. The prognosis was determined that I should have been found dead or dead before reaching the emergency room. My right lung is still healing because it was not getting any oxygen, and I was on oxygen for two and half years October 2011 is when the doctor took me off the oxygen. With all the chaos running around putting in IVs and giving me shots of blood thinners, something or someone inside of me kept me going, like being in a movie that was not real. I was not afraid because of my faith and determination and I did not feel as if I was going to die. I remember the doctor telling my family how strong I was, but it was just God holding my hand through it all. My family was in tears even though I was trying to comfort them, I could see how scared they appeared in their eyes for me. Yes and No I should have died over a month before I went into the hospital. The point is that God saved my life on Easter Sunday, the day he rose from the dead. I believe God chooses our day to die, some die young and some die old, but all along God is still in control. Father in Jesus name Amen

Prayer of Thanks

A statue built, a picture painted, an image created.
I don't need an idol to worship God.
I can bow down on my knees or just bow my head anytime of the day and pray, God will still hear me.
I don't know what God, Jesus, the Holy Ghost or Mary looks like.
I don't need to see their faces.
Too feel the love that they have for me.
Jesus walks in my soul and my heart is in love with God for every moment of my life.
I thank you God for everyday you have given me to breathe.
I thank God for giving us Mary that gave us the Joy of Gods Heart Jesus.
I believe in God the Father, the Son and the Holy Ghost with everything in me.
I thank you God for always being there at everyplace, every turn, every stop and every moment with us.
We are always in need of you God.
The only thing I have done right in my life is truly love you God, with every part of my heart.
God I thank you, for blessing my steps,
because when I get lost they will always lead me back to you everyday of my life.
Just walk with God, just to see were he takes you, Thank you God.
In Jesus name, Amen

Prayer of Thanks 1

Songs of my heart lyrics of love

Everyday, every minute, every hour and every moment the love of my heart belong too you Lord.
I have a song in my heart for you God.
Every breath of my life I feel your melody running in my soul.
You are my peace of mind that carries me with your love.
All through my life I been singing the songs of my heart lyrics of love to you God,
God you are the rhythm that breathes the life into my heart every morning,
You are the voice that sings a song making my soul dance for you,
You are the smile that moves all the tears to the side filling my heart with your laughter,
You are the gift my soul has been blessed with, a song that sing in me forever,
I Love you, God.
You are the song that is the key to open my heart to you,
You are the Songs of my heart lyrics of love.
In Jesus name, Amen

2

Thank you

Thirsting for your love craving too feel your embrace in my heart.

Holy divine is my Lord all my love every part is devoted to your heart.

Almighty, amazing love pouring like a shower of rain down into my heart.

Never felt such a tender spirit causing my love to desires a place Lord in your heart.

Kind, gentle my precious kiss of love, which the Lord has cherished in His heart.

Yearning, longing for just a touch of your love Lord here every moment wrapped around my heart.

Only you Lord can uncover my soul and release the joy of my love into your heart.

Understanding the power of your presence, that follows every step of my heart.

Lord let my love ignite in your heart, Thank you Lord.
In Jesus Name Amen

3

God I apologize

For all the sin I have done in your eyes.
I admire a Father that doesn't leave His child.
When I ran down the wrong road, you gave chase.
You took my hand. Open my eye.
To help me to see clearly what stand before me.
I request to stand with you God everyday of my life.
When I had doubted you in my mind, you showed up too saved my life.
You are the blessing that lives inside my soul.
For all the times I have washed my hands in unclean waters.
Please forgive me, God I apologize.

For each tear that fall from your eyes cause of me.
A good Father, that keeps His child from leave the yard.
When I start straddling the fence, you lift me up.
Open my eyes to see want is really on the other side.
I will let everything in me express the love for you in my heart.
Today Lord you can rip away all the love in me and I will still love you even more tomorrow.
I know you were there to save my life from me; you are the blessing that woke up in my soul.
For all the time I turn my back on you when you needed a helping hand.
Please forgive me, God I apologize.

For forgiving your child for all the lies that was said.
I knew that I wasn't right as I look you in the eye.
Judge by the love of a Father that is always ready too forgive His child.
You hold me tight, open my eyes.
God has been in me all my life. I see how much love gather itself in your heart for me.
No matter how my day go by. I just hope your always home God waiting for me.
You are the one that came and save me from myself.
You are the blessing that left your smile in my soul.
For all that I have done wrong when I though no one was looking.
Please forgive me, God I apologize.

For all the shameful things I have done before your eyes.
God you kept your breath in me and Father you save my life.
I am so graceful. To know that I'm loved by God with more love then I could every love him with.
You hold me tight, open my eyes. To see how much God has watch over my life.
He keeps mending his heart with love and forgiveness that he has for us sinners.
I watched the love in me heal every part of His heart.
For all the sins we think God can't see. I hold His broken heart in my heart.
I am so proud to see the love that God has in His heart for me.
You are the hero that saved my life today. You are the blessing that spoke to my soul.
I apologize for every moment I used right to hide my wrongs.
Please forgive me, God I apologize.
In Jesus name, Amen

4

Welcome Love

Welcome Love, Welcome Salvation.
For His presence is always here.
Running around me, too save me from all and myself.
Every moment you have been setting here beside me.
Lord just always find away too be here for me in my life.

Welcome Love, Welcome Trials and Tribulations.
For His presence move all those who test my love for Him.
I am in distress stuck in trouble waters that bring stress to my life.
He has washed away the pain life has placed in me.
He has cleaned my soul of its sins.

Welcome Love, Welcome Bewildered Soul.
For His presence is the light that leads me.
I'm never lost or will ever be unable to find my way.
His spirit always guide's me everyday.

Welcome Love, Welcome Burdens.
For His presence is the hand that lifted all the weight off my shoulders.
Helping me to carry my life down the path God prepared every step for me.
He is always waiting at the in of the road to greet me.

Welcome Love, Welcome Deep Sorrow.
His presence is the arms that comfort my grief.
Replace my frown with his smile.
A gentle hug. Which dried my painful tears.
He relieve me now am free.

Welcome Love, Welcome Hidden Heart.
Instead of walking I kept trapping over my heart. Only God knows what to do with your hidden heart,
He has saved me from so much pain. Shield my heart from being broken.
To all those that were waiting too see me fall. God caught my life before I fell and broke apart.
His kindness come calling; His tender heart hold's me while I walk through life.
For His presence has found my heart wounding around in His love.
Welcome Love, Welcome God.
In Jesus Name Amen

5

Me

I'm the Almighty one.
There is no love like me.
Everything that come's from me is good.
My heart is filled with love.
The glory of love is within me.
You can always count on my love and me.
You are apart of my heart and me.
I will wash your soul with my mercy.
Come live in me and I will breathe your life through me.
My blood still runs from the cross drowning your sins everyday in me.
Thank you for believing in me with your whole heart.
The truth is that I am the son and through me God will set you free from all your sins.
You can't save yourself without me.
Hold my hand, let your life keep holding on to me.
Forgiveness is always calling from the voices of all Gods children.
My tender love melts at the sound of their cries.
Every step they take will be with me.
All your burdens are placed on my shoulders.
I will carry them for you everyday of your life.
Every face you see there you will always find me.
My love follows you into my heart.
A friend that is always there everywhere you go is me.
My heart is greedy when it comes to love.
My love will never leave you behind.
Your love will never depart from me if that's the way you want it to be.
Keep your focus on me, watch me, and believe in me to be there before you call.
Put all your energy in trusting me.
You set in the presence of my love and me forever.
It is me the Savior, Jesus Christ the one, God's joy is me.
In Jesus name Amen

6

Love

Your love sleeps in my heart.
Awake in my soul everyday.
My love completely pours out to you Lord.
Love that sacrificed everything just too be apart of me.
Like the sun light's up the world your love light's up my heart.
Love is my companion a relationship that brought me closer to God.
My heart chooses to love you Jesus with my whole heart.
My love finally caught your love waiting for me with open arms.
I want to keep seeing your love surround my life.
I want to feel every touch of love you have given my soul.
Lord forever can you lay your love down in my heart with you at it side.
You are the love my heart has never known could be so gentle.
Love is the most precious when it comes from God.
I shell cherish your love Jesus forever in my heart.
Lord blessed me with all the love my life desires.
Jesus you are the only one that has the key to my heart.
God know all the secret entrances into my heart.
My love destination is to find your heart God.
To let my love live forever in your peace.
Love you Jesus; Love you God, with all of me.
In Jesus name Amen

7

Praise God

Praise God.
I give Him all my heart and with all the breath that I breathe in me.
God is the Most High; He is the beginning and the end.
For the love He pours out for me.
He placed His mercy down on my path.
The strength He gave to guide me home to His arms.

Praise God.
Just love Him through the bad and good times with our whole heart.
Hold on, life is always going to shake you up a little.
When it comes to your heart there is no higher love than God.
That makes your soul float into His arms.
You are still breathing by the grace of His power.
For the word given to teach me His will.
The goodness of His heart gives my life direction.
The light of kindness of His heart has shown us how to find our way home.

Praise God.
I thank you Father, for all the days I have breath.
For all the days that sickness has passed me by.
The faces that you gave me to love, everyone of them remind me of you my God.
For the Forgiveness He has for my sins.
The blessing He has given me all my life has brought me home to His arms.
In Jesus name, Amen

8

Love

My heart would brake for the first time if I lost your love.
Life could not live in me if you stop breathing in me.
Love has grown up every day in my heart with you God.
My Savior planted His love in me the day before I was born.
I find myself lost in your love every moment of my life.
Your love breathes in and out of my soul.
My love bows to your presence as it lifts my spirit up into your loving arms.
You make my tears fall from the joy you placed in my heart.
I love that your love holds me close everyday in my life.
God your love keeps me near to always be there to save me from myself.
Protect my love let it embrace your heart.
Love can't walk alone without you Lord holding its hand.
You are the biggest part of my love.
I'll give it all up, sacrificed everything just to lay my love forever in your heart my Lord.
My heart is the companion for your love Lord.
God you are the teacher that taught my heart how to love.
My heart belongs to your love every moment that I breathe.
Everyday that I live my heart, my love I give it all to you God.
In Jesus name amen

9

Life

When I open my eyes, Lord I want you to be the first smile I see.
Jesus you are the face.
That lights up the world for me.
I appreciate your life wanting to breathe your life in me.
You are the sunshine that carries me down my path.
You are the hand that keeps me from falling in my life.
I can't stand on my own without you being my foundation.
I shall follow your foot steps down this road every day of my life.
I need you Lord, to always find time to hold me every moment I breathe.
Prepare my soul to feel every part of your love.
I walk not in the dark but in the light of your heart.
Lord may I see the world through your eyes.
Then I will know the right steps to take every day in my life.
Thank you for letting your joy lay down his life upon the cross.
To a world of sinners you gave your heart.
Lord here goes my heart with every part of my love.
My spirit can't live a minute without you living in me.
You make my spirit cry because I feel the presence of your glory moving in me.
Every tear that drop from my eyes falls in the center of your heart.
So I will pour all my love into your heart forever Lord.
We should never try to change someone belief about God. Always let them worship him in there our way.
Because we are all headed in the same direction we are all trying to receive the blessing to live in Gods house.
If you don't believe in God, than you need to move on in your on life.
 If we could go back in life follow every feet step we ever took.
We would be able to see all those beautiful smiles and all the frowns that walked with us in our lives.
All the tears that watched the pain run down from our eyes.
Everyone and everything that ever made us laugh.
It would be a blessing to know how many steps it took us in our life to get too God.
All those prayers we whispered to God in our lives.
Just to bring our love a little closer to God's heart.
God thank you for opening you heart, letting your beautiful love runaway with my heart everyday of my life.
In Jesus name Amen

10

At your side forever

Question you when I should have been questing myself.
Not following your directions.
In my life everything that has gone wrong I put the blame on you.
Trying too do it all on my own and I failed every time without you Lord guiding the way.
Stop praying to you was the biggest mistake I made in my life.
Climbing the mountain just too fall.
 Because my strength was not strong enough too pull me up without the power of God.
Not strong enough to move that rock that is chained to my life.
Lord I could not knock down those walks that stood in my way everyday.
Every door I tried to open was locked before me because I lost that special key God gave to me.
No one answer when I called all my friends seem to be hiding in there on shame.
I asked but I did not lesson to your voice I went my on way.
I got lost taking steps blindly in the dark with out your light.
I thought you lift me until I felt your hand touch mine.
I can feel my soul leaping into you arms Lord.
I finally found that lost key waiting in side of me God.
God my heart ache for the joy of your love,
Through all the dark, every day of my life the only one I truly missed was you God.
My life is so grateful to have you at my side forever.
In Jesus name Amen

11

Lord I

Lord I have secured your love in my heart.
I locked my heart away forever from this world.
Lord you are the only one that has the key to open my heart.
To see how your love flows around in me.
Let the power of your love favor my soul brings me closer to your heart.
Lock my love away in your arms God.

Lord I refuge to let go of the safety of your hand.
I am afraid that I will get lost if your love stops guiding me.
I forever grow in your peacefulness.
Favor me with your love everyday of my life.
Lord I approach your throne with the gift of my soul.
My spirit bows down forever to your grace.
While my soul continues to give you praise.
Abundantly I give you Lord my love forever.

Lord I depend on you to follow me down this path you have prepared for me.
I want you Lord, to control my every step.
Cause I want you to be the shelter to shield me from the storms.
You are the light that light's up the darkness in my life.
Lord you freed me with your love from all my fears forever.

Lord I thank you for my thankful heart.
Too have the will to live by your faith, truth and hope.
God my love keeps my heart looking for you always. Allowing my life too believe in you forever.
I am wrapped in your warm mercy. Lord I hold you above all my needs.
I lay my love down at your feet my life rejoice in your arms.
Please God, anoint my life with your love forever.
In Jesus name Amen

12

Each and everyday

Lord you are the friend that is always here to pick me up when I fall each and everyday.

A shoulder too lay my head on; you are the prayer that carry me each and everyday.

You are the light that taught me to find my way out of the dark each and everyday.

You are the breath that touches me to wake up to the smile on your face each and everyday.

Lord you are the love that keeps my heart humbled and growing in your joy each and everyday.

You are the hand that walks me down a safe, secure path with every step each and everyday.

You are the teacher that taught my heart love and you have laid your truth across my tongue to speak each and everyday.

What my soul needs is to never get lost and always find away home back into Gods merciful arms each and everyday.
In Jesus name Amen

13

He is you are

He is you are the answer to those unsolved question that lie in me everyday.

He is you are the light that finds my way everyday.

He is you are the anointed oil that is pour over my soul everyday.

He is you are the breath that breathes life in me everyday.

He is you are the love that encouraged my heart to love everyday.

He is you are the ministry that preaches in me everyday.

He is you are the blood that runs from the cross into my veins everyday.

He is you are the mercy that continues to hold me in your arms everyday.

He is you are the presence that lives with me everyday.

He is you are the joy that favors me in His heart everyday.

He is you are the song, the melody that sings your love song in me everyday.

He is you are the key that opens all doors that stand before me everyday.

He is you are the need, the want that bless me with you everyday.

He is you are the opened ears that hear all our prayers everyday.

He is you are the Savior, the protector that surrounds me everyday.

He is you are the hand that always there to pick me up when I fall everyday.

He is you are the strength that lifts me up into your arms everyday.

He is you are the beautiful life that lay down by our side all day and night everyday.

He is you are the soft voice that speaks to my heart and all the good that rolls off my tongue everyday.

He is you are the life running from my heart into my soul laughing all the way everyday.

He is you are my precious Lord God, Jesus Christ our Savior standing next to me everyday.
In Jesus name Amen

14

Love

Love when you wake me up everyday.

Love how I hold you in my heart.

Love I see you walk into my life.

Love I am blessed to know how it feels when I lay in the mercy of your arms.

Love when your presence wraps around me.

Love how your love soaks itself into me.

Love you are every part of my heart,

Love I love how it feels when your joy lay down with me in your arms.

Love when you take every step with my soul.

Love how every moment you embrace my life with yours.

Love your love is always there for me.

Love I love how it feels when I lay in your gentle arms.

Love your love has found away into my heart.

Love it is good when you lead the way in my life.

Love how you never let go of my heart.

Love how you walk into the room and leave your smile.

Love you are the need and every want in my life.

Love I hope you always want you to be apart of me.
In Jesus name Amen

15

And you hold me everyday

I just want to stare at the smile on your glorious face and you hold me everyday.

You are the scent of a morning rose blooming in the early morning sun and you hold me everyday.

You are the clean air after the rain storm has passed and you hold me everyday.

You are the quiet moment that a wakes when it seem like the world has stop moving and you hold me everyday.

You are the most beautiful sensory my eyes have ever seen in my life and you hold me everyday.

You are the glory I see just before I open my eyes each morning and you hold me everyday.

You are the sun raise that takes away the darkness in my life and you hold me everyday.

You are the brightness noon that light up a lost soul's way home and you hold me everyday.

You are the shelter that keeps me safe, the shield of protection that covers me throughout my life and you hold me everyday.

I safely lay down in your presence Lord, I finally found my peace of mind in you and you hold me everyday.

God you shared what you love with my heart, Jesus you quickly invited my soul into your arms and you hold me everyday.

There is no another arms I rather have holding me, it must be you everyday God and you hold me everyday.
In Jesus Name, Amen

16

Love

My love forever flows abundantly into your heart God.
Just the sound of your name Jesus takes control of my life.
When your presence enters the room my soul jumps for joy.
Glory that run through my soul into my heart.
Wrapping itself around all the love I have for you Jesus.
Jesus fills me up with life and peace, because you are the one that died to set me free.
There is no boundary for how much of my heart you can have.
God my love recycles itself over and over in your heart, my love live in you.
Jesus' love doesn't have a limit or a switch that turns His love off and on.
His love grows every minute in me feeding my heart throughout my life.
Joy is the heart that gave His life upon the cross.
That sets beside me everyday.
God is holding my hand as I walk with Him through life.
It's a pleasant feeling in the air when you are around Lord.
He walked into my life and gave me His love.
My love is calling you God with every breath of my heart.
Jesus you are my hunger that feeds my soul.
God you are drowning my heart with your love in my life.
My life has desired your love every moment Jesus.
I trust my love to follow your heart with ever step God.
Always a Savior in my life, love you God, love you Jesus forever.
In Jesus name Amen

17

Joy of my heart, thank you Lord, thank you God

We must stop and look at are own selves before we judge someone else life trust God.
Before we judge try too look through the eyes of God.
Before we get lost in the dark were there is no light to be found call on God.
We should call on you Lord, before thing starts too go wrong and you can't find your way to God.
All my problems seem to come at me all at once, time to seek God.
When it rains it pours but I found my shelter in God.

Joy of my heart, thank you Lord, thank you God

When it seems like nothing is going right we must learn too hold on to God.
Everything I touch seems to fall apart giving me the blues I need the touch of God.
There are times when the evil one will stand in your way, please depend on the power of God.
Your so call friends will talk about you and leave you on your own, find your true friend in God.
Never put me down, always around and stand forever at my side, His name is God.

Joy of my heart, thank you Lord, thank you God

I knock there seem to be no answer until I here His voice say come in child and there I found God.
Walking down this path alone I would have found myself lost again, until I ask you to walk with me God.
There is no secure place as safe as the arms of God.
I still trap over my own two feet, slap sometimes but your hand reaches out to catch me every time God.
You travel that road that seems to have no end and I'm so tried until I fall into the open arms of God.

Joy of my heart, thank you Lord, thank you God
In Jesus name Amen

18

Love

Love falls upon my heart every moment of my life.
His presence follows me everyday.
My love desires to please Him in anyway He wish.
His joy and love wraps around my heart.
Unconditionally love has been pour over my heart.
My love has enslaved my heart to God.
I bow down my love and my soul at your feet.
His spirit direct every step my love makes.
Enabling my heart too walk on the same path that His love has walked.
Lord you are all I have there will be no other hero for me.
There is no one that loves me with there whole heart like you Lord.
My love is for your arms only.
My heart worships your every word.
Through your love I learn to be grateful.
It is a blessing to set in the gentle hands of your love that holds me forever.
My heart is happy to be griped in your love God.
Grasping power of love that holds me so tight comes right on time when my heart calls to him.
Lord your love makes it so hard to breathe, because your love smothers the air in my heart.
You are the love my heart has given itself too forever.
In Jesus name Amen,

19

God is good

Trial and tribulation has tested our faith in God.
You have lost your salvation some were on the road.
To give up on life as we feel our lives already stuck in sinking sand.
Hold on to that rock that will give you the strength to pull yourself out of anything.
God is good.

Your foundation has cracked your soul.
Sorrow has touched your heart too try to break the bond between you and God.
The more you struggle with your life you are still stuck in sinking sand.
Hold on to that rock that will give you the strength to pull yourself out of anything.
God is good.

He grows in my heart like a blooming flower.
He flows in my soul like a water fall that never ends.
He walked me through my sorrows.
He dries my tears before they fall from my eyes.
He fed me when I was hungry with His glory.
He gave me drink when my soul was thirsty.
He comforts me when I was lonely with His touch.
He gave me the answers for all my questions about life and Him.
He caught me before I slipped and fell from His grace.
Yes, God is good.
In Jesus name, Amen

20

Love

My heart pours out its thanks at your feet Lord.
I feel his love messing around in my heart.
His love is like a birds wing flying in me.
God you touch my spirit everywhere gently.
He holds the hand of my soul.
Everywhere I look I see His love.
My heart is so thankful for his joy falls in me like an endless waterfall.
It is a blessing knowing you are always here to love me.
Your arms gentle wrap my love in your heart.
My heart freely give it's self to your love.
I put my love, along with my soul into your heart just for you to keep with you Lord forever.
I want to breathe in your goodness.
Cause I want your love and your thankfulness to grow every moment in me.
Let my love walk forever beside you everyday of my life.
Love you God.
In Jesus name Amen

21

I Trust

I trust you Lord with every part of my being.
I will lay down my soul in the pulse of your hand Lord.
I know you will watch over me every moment life breathes in me.
Fear no evil for your presence surround every part of me.
Fear no day that comes with many burdens for your strength carries me through it all.
Your hands guided me out of every situation that falls upon me.
I trust in Him that I will succeed in everything I touched or do.
I believe you Lord will always be here before I am in need of you.
There not a heart or a love that is so reliable than the Lords.
My spirit is depending on the Lord to lead me in the right direction.
Allowing your gentle hands too touch my soul with your grace.
You are the love the supreme power roaming in my heart.
The trust in my heart has made you my world.
Hope walk in because of you Lord can be trusted with every step I take.
My faith has grown to trust you every moment with my life.
A Good day, a bad day, I will always trust you to be the peace in me.
I Trust you always God.
In Jesus name Amen,

22

In Me

Life has stumbled over my faith until I felt the power of your presence flowing freely in me.

Life had faltered my steps until I felt your grasping power grip too my hand leading every step in me.

Life has struggled with my heart until I felt the power of your hope running like a river in me.

Life has empty my heart until I felt the strength of your powerful love ignite in me.

Life has darkened my path until I felt the power of your light start burning bright in me.

Life has silence my prayers until I felt God wake up my life with His joy our Savior Jesus Christ He move's in me.

Life has stress out my will until I felt the power of your comfort lay upon my shoulder, as you wrapped your gentle arms around me, as your love melts in me.

Life has angered my Spirit until I felt the power of your voice humble every part of me, helping me to find the peace in me.

Life has built many walks and placed so many rocks in my way until I felt the power of your will knocking down those walks, moving all the rocks that stood before me and you are the key to open all the doors that hide in me.

Life has walked me here to face the love in my heart, to wake up my love and see the one that gave me His love upon a cross
blood that still flows in me, giving my heart your everlasting love in me.
In Jesus name Amen

23

Love

You are the stream of love that runs wild down from the mountain over the hill top kissing the grown everywhere.

Running over the face of the rock, that keeps giving me strength.

Washing away the walls, that has built them selves around my life.

This stream has found it way from deep in the dark into the light.

Filling up an old dried up pond with all your gratefulness.

The stream because a river filled with your love for me,

That keeps on moving for many miles like tears that running down from your eyes.

Quietly moving like a lonely heart that lost its love.

Love rush down in me falling into my heart like a beautiful waterfall.

Racing into the lake's waiting arms, to embrace your life with mine.

Breathing new life every place you touch in me.

Water of life has it on spirit that thirst for more of you God to pour into my life.

As I float alone my soul feels your peace enter me.

My love falls into your wide open river like rain drop from a cloud up high.

The river in me flows along way just to find the ocean of your wide open heart Lord God.

I shall lie forever on your beach of love for every moment of my life.

I just want you God to be the ocean of love that flows and lives forever in me.

In Jesus name Amen

24

Moment to Moment

You are my love, life and hope.
My heart would burst just at the sound of your name.
God your name echoes over and over in my soul.
I can hear the whispers of your name in the wind.
Because as I breathe I feel you move around in me moment to moment.

The presence of God holds me in His arms.
I would have no life if you take your love from me Lord.
Stop breathing if your say you don't want to be here anymore.
My heart, my soul and my love would die if you walked out of my life.
Then I want feel you move anymore in me moment to moment.

You are my love, life and hope.
My heart pours out its love to you everyday I live.
I feel your love walk into the room.
God made His presence known by touching my heart with His love.
I feel your Holy Spirit hold me moment to moment.

If I wonder down this lonely road and get lost.
But if for some reason you don't come to find me Lord.
I would be loss in the dark forever without your guidance in my life.
If you Lord turn a deaf ear to my prayers how would I find the right answers I need.
There is not minute I can go on without you in my life moment to moment.

You are my love, life and hope.
My life depends on you Lord to guide every step I take.
Every piece of my heart love's every part of you God.
Jesus you are the life that lives every day in my soul.
I lay every part of my love in your hands of hope.
Thank you God for letting my love, life and hope breathe forever in you moment to moment.
In Jesus name Amen,

25

Thank You

Thank you, God for walking with me everyday.
Your always right on time to lead my life you have been here to guide me.
I can always depend on you to be there God.
Side by side in life, I feel every moment when your presence takes every step with me.
Your arms are my shelter from harm.
You are always protecting me from all the storms that I must face throughout my life.
Breathing your life in me gives my soul its peace.
I feel good to live my life in God he is the strength in me.
I can't lose my way or get lost if you are my direction.
You are always holding my hand day and night throughout my life.
I pray I will never let go of your hand, even if thing go wrong and in since like there is no air for me to breathe.
I will stay strong until I find the breath that you Lord breathes in me.
I will never let go my grip would even get tighter as I step through life.
Because no matter what is going on in my life I know you will always be my hero.
Thank you, God for never letting go of my life.
In Jesus name Amen,

26

You

You are the light I love to see breathe life in me.
Hope smiles at me every morning.
Lay your glory upon my shoulder.
Carry my life away with you.
Bring me your joy.
Pour it in my heart to wakeup my love.
Give me your merciful hand.
Walk with me down my path of life,
Always let your grace stand beside me.
I need your presence to follow my every step.
Your Holiness meets me around every corner I turn.
All my trust is given to you as a gift.
I travel down this rugged road guided by Thee.
I see your peace waiting for me.
Divine love hold's me while I move on in my life.
Together we shall walk my soul into your gentle open arms.
Every moment in my life I will stand with you Jesus.
My love has always been there in your heart for safe keeping.
Jesus I give you my life direct my steps forever with God.
I Jesus name Amen

27

Smile

When I feel loss I find you setting next to me.
You always have such a beautiful smile on your face.
Jesus you make everything in my life ok.
Nothing is too difficult for me now God.
I'm not afraid to walk down this rocky road.
I just picture those smiles that always stand next to me.
All my worries they have took and hide them from me.
Sorrows don't have apart in my life anymore.
Their smiles are stuck forever in my mind.
They are the power in me to knock down walks.
To move all the rock that stakes up against me.
The strength that it gives me I can conquer anything that stands before me.
I used their smiles to light the path I walk in my life.
Jesus you have been more than a shoulder of comfort for me.
It is a blessing to be able to give your whole heart to God.
I wrap up my soul with my love as a gift to them.
Everyday I open my eyes I see those warm smiles breathe out of me.
I feel so grateful that they took time to show me how to believe in them.
Following those beautiful smiles has kept me on the right path.
But trusting in those smiles has been the answer to my life.
In Jesus name Amen

28

Here

Here I give you all of me.
Lord you have walked me beyond my limitation.
I travel this road without hesitation.
I know that your presence watch over me with every step I take.
My heart has connected with your love my Lord.
My love has chain it self to your heart Jesus.
I approach this new day in search of God.
No longer tied down with these earthly shackles God has set me free.
Everyplace I go and everyplace I am. I am always focusing on God.
I want to be blessed with your presence God every moment of my life.
To grow in you God is my most desire in my soul.
He is the way, the life and the truth, that keep my spirit headed into His arms.
My life has attaché itself to the joy of God.
I have turn over my life to God I shall live right here forever by His will.
Here Lord I give you ever part of me.
In Jesus name Amen

29

Let your forgiveness set me free

The sun comes up, the sun goes down.
Some days I can't get up lying here watching my life drain away.
My heart is so heavy can't move anymore my life is so tried of carrying these burdens.
They have brought me to my knees. I pray too be free, Oh Lord.
From all of my burdens that lay upon my shoulders.
That is breaking the back of my soul and my spirit walks in pain.
With all these burdens set on my shoulders weighting me down.
Lift me up, Standby me and help me Lord.
Let your forgiveness set me free.

The sun comes up, the sun goes down.
Some days I can't get up setting here watching my life pass me by.
My heart is so heavy can't move anymore my life is so tried. My life has worn me down.
I don't have the strength anymore to carry these burdens.
They have brought me to my knees.
I pray too be free, Oh Lord.
From all of my burdens that cling to me that eats away at my soul.
Trying to make my heart loss hope, trying to pull my spirit down.
Lift me up, Standby me and help me Lord.
Let your forgiveness set me free.

The sun comes up, the sun goes down.
Some days I can't get up because it's hard to look in the mirror at my life.
My burdens I have built so high now they have fallen down around my life.
My heart is so heavy. Can't move anymore my life is so tried.
Lost the well to get up and walk on my own.
Looking for away to heal my pain.
They have brought me to my knees. I pray too be free, Oh Lord.
Thinking I did not need you Lord to help me carry these burdens.
My spirit has gotten loss and darkness has blinded my eyes from the light.
Trying to move my life forward has me wondering on this winding road.
My burdens have covered up the light you lit in me.
My burdens get heavier day to day, Lord I lay all burdens down at your feet.
Catch me because I just might fall down again.
Lift me up, Standby me and help me Lord.
Let your forgiveness set me free.
In Jesus name Amen

30

I can't live without you Lord

I want to see you walk into my life everyday.
The first thing I want to see when I open my eyes is your face Lord.
You have grown forever in my heart.
Lord I have loved you more than life has breathed in me.
I was born with my soul lying in your arms.
My spirit is covered with your love Lord.
I breathe because you Lord desired to live in me.
I hope everyday of my life is wrapped in your heart.
I pray that your mercy find a home in me.
Lord set me in your grace that I may always be found in your favor.
Your joy has lived everyday in my heart.
Your smile touches my spirit now it laughs forever.
My faith in you believes that all my needs will be met.
Your praise chases hallelujah in and out of my soul.
Day by day your love checks on my heart.
Lord your glory follows me every moment.
The sound of your voice echo's around in my soul.
Your Holiness walks me home to your waiting arms.
Oh Lord, at the end of the day.
When I lay down to sleep I want you to be the last face I see just before I close my eyes.
It good to know I can't live without you, Lord.
In Jesus name Amen

31

I believe in prayer

I believe in prayer.
Even when you don't answer them all, I still believe in you.
You always here with the answer for every step that helped me in life.
Those prayers that holds me, keeps me on the right path.
You are the prayers that lights up my way through the darkness in my life.
The prayers that invited your presence too come into my life everyday.

I believe in prayer.
Lord you are the prayer that can always violate my free will anytime.
I pray that you walk into my life even when I not looking.
Everyday I need you all time to be standing here by my side.
Free will has run away the day I lay my life in your hands.
I pray that my heart forever choices to love you beyond my life Lord.
I gave up all my freedom when I followed your foot steps into your arms.
I have prayed to free myself for all worldly things when I gave you my life.

I believe in prayer.
I have faced all my problems I pray too you Lord to clear my mind.
My soul is feeling down I pray too you Lord to lift my burden.
My mind needs rest from thinking to much about if God will answer my prayer.
I need to find a peaceful place for my soul to set down and pray.
Together we can handle what ever life brings us every day with a prayer.
In your presence my life has set permanent residence in you.
I will pray Lord that you bring my life above my needs.
I pray to you God that I give you my all.
I believe in prayer. I believe in God.
In Jesus name Amen

32

Heart

When I first met you God I fall in love with your heart.
Your love feels like rain storm going off in my heart.
You greeted me with love so much that it smoother my heart.
My love has lost it freedom being capture by your heart.
Lord your have such a rare love my heart and my love wants to be apart of your heart.
I value every moment your presence surrounds my heart.
Lord you are worthy to have every part of my heart.
There is nothing more precious then Gods loving heart.
When my life faces uncertainty my worries walked into the arms of your heart.
I cherished everyday you hold me in the love of your heart.
Without doubt I have found the love that I need in my life living in my heart.
You Lord have shown me your desirable heart.
Everyday my love draws closer to your heart.
You touch my love by running your hand across my heart.
Where no one has ever been, your love has been found there such a beautiful love deep in my heart.
I cannot resist the love that poured from your heart.
Love breathes like an old spirited wine that never loses its taste for the heart.
When you breathe your love into me my love faints into your heart.
My soul is inspired with hope running out of my heart.
May God catch every drop of love that over spills out of my heart.
God love grows in all place, every crack in my heart.
Lord I am so happy that you endure my love to be in your heart.
I am so glade that you bless me with your heart.
How generous you are for letting my love lives in your heart.
Thank you God for every moment your love has bless my heart with love from your heart.
In Jesus name Amen

33

Seek You

Each morning I awake I seek your face my Lord.
Will you prepare me Lord for whatever comes my way on this day?
You have taught me how to walk down this path.
My eyes are open wide to see were my footsteps will carry me.
I hold your hand with a tightly grip.
There no way I would be able to let myself let go of your hand.
Because I wear the strength you clothed me with everyday of my life.
I can stand-up to any situation that life brings my way.
Grasping my life to your every word has prepared me.
Too not let uncertainty lead my life down the wrong way.
I ask you Lord to let your Holy Spirit renewal itself in me.
Lord let your presence communicate with my soul everyday of my life.
My heart is unrelenting for your love.
Your gentle touch has found my heart.
Your precious mercy follows me everyday.
I am so happy to be covered in your joy.
As my mind fall asleep in your peaceful arms.
Each night just before I close my eyes I still seek your face my Lord.
In Jesus name Amen

34

Nothing comes between me and God

Blessed by God's unapproachable light, I shall always dwell in the arms of God.
He is my protector and my Savior every moment of my life.
Nothing comes between me and God

I just don't need Him when things are going bad, but every waking moment I breathe.
I need you to always be near to keep my soul safe.
Nothing comes between me and God

Anoint me with your presence everyday.
Respond to my love by bring me closer to your heart.
You are the lighted pathway that shows me the way to you God.
Nothing comes between me and God

No one measure up to your love Lord.
Your heart stands alone when it comes to a passionate heart.
I'm so proud that you are the provision for my needs.
Nothing comes between me and God

I depended on God to being me closer to His heart.
Feeling overwhelmed with His power and glory.
Not even in my darkness hours could separate me from God.
I will forever hold on to His hand beyond time.
Nothing comes between me and God

God you are found in every situation that comes before me.
That's why I enjoy being in your presence every day.
God you have made it where my heart easily loves's you.
Thank you for being with me.
 For watching over me you are constantly the missing peace of love that I need in my life.
Earthly love will come and go but your love God will never let me go.
Nothing comes between me and God
In Jesus name Amen

35

I don't care

He's the voice that softly whispers my name.
That wakes me every morning.
His strength carries me everyday.
His hand is the one that guides me down the path of my life.
I don't care if you don't love God.
I don't care if you don't believe in Jesus.
Because I got Him right here in my heart, in my soul, moving all around inside of me.
He is every part of me, I eat and I breathe every drop of His presence everyday of my life.

Just thinking of Him, He can make a bad day go a different way.
When His presence walks into the room all sins are forgiven.
He touches my soul like no one has ever touched me. He fills me with so much hope.
I pray that he is away here in my life to show me the way.
I shall not be move for the power of our Mighty God stands with me.
I don't care if you don't want to hear about God.
I don't care if you don't want to know Jesus.
Because I got Him right here in my heart, in my soul, moving all around inside of me.
He is every part of me, I eat and I breathe every drop of His presence everyday of my life.

He took the pain that I carry to long, pulled right out of me, setting me free.
There not a moment in my life I don't need you Lord.
Once there was loneness then I found a place in your arms to lay my soul.
I trust every step that I take with you God.
I know I will be lead to my peace.
There I will rest before a new day start my life all over again.
I open my eyes my friend is here waiting to walk me through a new day once again.
I don't care if you talk bad about God.
I don't care if you stop praying to Jesus.
Because I got Him right here in my heart, in my soul, moving all around inside of me.
He is every part of me, I eat and I breathe every drop of His presence everyday of my life.
In Jesus name Amen

36

Mighty God

I just want to set quietly in the presence of my Mighty God.
I need you to be the one that's maps out my path every step I take in my life.
My love has a deep yeaning to meet your heart.
I am so thankful that you have inviting your love into my heart.
Your gentle touch runs across my soul.
Healing all the pain we hide deep inside our lives.
Lord I hand over all my problems to be fixed by your Holy hands.
Let your power show me how to handle everything wrong that stand before me.
Your presence poured its light into the darkness part of my life.
To wake up my sins to show them that joy and forgiveness has move into my soul.
Your presence stands guard over my soul now
Continually you fulfill the needs in every part of my being.
Your promise is always there before I ask, right on time.
We make such a mess of our lives when we try to direct our on journeys.
But alone come's God with His Mighty hand to guide us back home again.
There will never be any other God before Thee.
Nothing is free in this world, but the love of God the Father, Jesus Christ our Savior and the Holy Ghost pure love.
They are always here, with open arms everyday in my life.
You don't have to pay for the most beautiful love you are forever going to feel in your heart.
That why I am always here wrapped in the love of my Mighty God's arms.
In Jesus name Amen

37

My Hallelujah

Every day I feel you breathe life into me, my Hallelujah.
I don't walk alone He's away here to take each step with me, my Hallelujah.
Seeking Him was my most important journey of my life to find, my Hallelujah.
I will bow down to no another but one, my Hallelujah.
I will spend every moment of my life in your presence, my Hallelujah.
Every inch of the day can you hold me, my Hallelujah?
Pour your joy in me fill me with all of you, my Hallelujah.
I put you in charge of my life, my Hallelujah.
I'm longing for your love to fall into my heart, my Hallelujah.
There are certain things we need in our lives and most of the time it's always you, my Hallelujah.
The sight of you lights up the darkness in me, my Hallelujah.
When I cry it is all about the joyful tears you put in my life, my Hallelujah.
I desire to please you and to do right by you, my Hallelujah.
I'm thrown into the arms of your gentle love, my Hallelujah.
I focus firmly on seeking your face all the time, my Hallelujah.
Your forgiveness has removed all my sins, my Hallelujah.
You have set my soul free into your glory, my Hallelujah.
It's good to feel your company set down next to me, my Hallelujah.
There nothing better than the love you have placed in my heart, my Hallelujah.
I am building up the peaceful walls that you help build around in my mind, my Hallelujah.
Every step you take to guide my life in the right direction, my Hallelujah.
Your whispers keep me going down the right path that you prepare for me, my Hallelujah.
I fell down quickly He picked me up; back on my feet he lifted me into his arms, my Hallelujah.
Blessed by your unapproachable light pulling me closer too you, my Hallelujah.
I will always dwell near Him for He is my protector, my Hallelujah.
He's my Savior for every moment I breathe in this life, my Hallelujah.
I love you every moment of the day, my Hallelujah.
You are every part of the love in my heart, the guardian of my soul and the light of my spirit, my Hallelujah.
In Jesus name Amen

38

With Him

When I die as my spirit walks away I don't want to see you cry for me.
When it's my time I will spread my wings and fly into His waiting arms.
Don't cry for me I'll be alright here with Him.
Don't be sad, because I'm gone.
Because where I'm going I'll be free.
Only grateful tear will fall from my eyes because I'm with Him.
Just dance and sing a sweet song for me child,
Sing a song that makes the hold room happy,
Just thank Him for every moment we spent in this life,
For all the times we laugh and cried together,
The hugs that put that beautiful smiles back on our faces,
Every day we prayed to make our lives closer to Him,
Walking in His presence,
Given Him every step we take,
Letting Him be every breath you breathe,
Giving Him complete control over your life,
Only wish I had done it sooner,
I believe I missed out on a lot of blessing,
But I am alright now here with Him,
It feels so good to be touch by His spirit,
He's leading me down the trial of glory,
To His most quit place,
Were I sit before the gates of haven waiting for judgment day with Him,
Here I am in good company,
Don't cry for me, enjoy your life and try to live it right,
Pray everyday to keep His presence always wrapped around you,
Let His will make all your decisions,
and let Him guide every step in your life.
 I'm alright because I'm where I want to be right here with Him.
In Jesus name Amen

39

Light

I pray Lord that you don't let the light of your spirit burn out in me.
I need your light to find my way through life.
I walk down the lighted path with every step taken in your direction.
Let your light reveal the hope you placed in my soul.
I confess that my sins have leaded me down the wrong way without your light.
I pray that the presence of your light walks with me on my journey in life.
Hold my hand Lord guide me with your Holy light.
God you are the gentle voice that lights up my heart with love.
You have built the light of your foundation in me.
You are the light of courage that carries me through all my stumbles, slips and falls in my life.
In my heart I feel you are always here letting your marvelous light shine in me.
Your song is the light that constantly sings in me.
Your righteousness has removed all my sins into the light.
Now I walk in the glory of your light.
Everyday I depend on your light to show me the way.
I trust that your light will always be there to walk me home.
I need your light to be able to always find my way to you Lord.
I hope you light up my life every moment I breathe.
I truly believe you are the light that my life needs.
Every turn I make, every step I take Lord I need your light here by my side every moment.
As long as your light is in me I can do anything because your life forever burns in me.
I can feel the warmth of your love lighting up my heart.
Keeping my soul feed by the light you shine forever in my life.
I hope Lord you don't let your candle ever burn out in me always light my way in my life.
In Jesus name Amen

40

God your, my heart

He is my weakness that takes over my soul.
When I first met you my heart shook.
I felt faint because your touch ran through my soul.
Then my love followed you into the waiting arms of your Holy Spirit.
I breathe every part of you into my heart constantly.
Glory loves me with every breath I breathe.
With every beat,
God your, my heart

He is the keeper of my soul.
God will always be the stowaway hidden in my heart.
He's the grip that never let go of my love.
Arms forever wrapped around my life.
A love that seems too rain in me constantly.
Glory loves me with every breath I breathe,
With every beat,
God your, my heart

He is the beautiful spirit that wakes up my soul.
I thank you God for all the loved ones you have place in my life.
Because every day I get too see your face God through all that love.
I need your love to keep living in my life constantly.
Glory loves me with every breath I breathe.
With every beat,
God your, my heart
In Jesus name Amen

41

My heart, my soul, and my life

God you have an undying love burning in my heart.
Father you are the one that rules every part of my soul.
Lord your good fortune blessed me with an everlasting light in my life.
Glory you have fulfilled my heart, my soul and my life with your living joy.

God you have a wonderful forever love pouring into my heart.
Father with your will you are in control of my soul.
Lord you have successfully walked me down the path of my life.
Glory your love has rejoiced in my heart, my soul and my life by you God manifesting yourself
in me.

God you have an endless love wondering around in my heart.
Father you make it known too me that you direct my soul.
Lord you have watched over my wellbeing everyday of my life.
Glory you are the one who conquered my heart, my soul and my life forever in your arms.
In Jesus name, Amen

42

Beautiful

Beautiful, your charm lives everywhere in my heart.

Beautiful, your hug embraces every part of my heart.

Beautiful, your grace is very pleasing to my heart.

Beautiful, your warm affection softly kisses my heart.

Beautiful, your gentle touch forever finds its way into my heart.

Beautiful, your elegance granted you entrance into my heart.

Beautiful, your kindliness selfishly made its bed in my heart.

Beautiful, your loveliness admires the love you created in my heart.

Beautiful, your tender arms seized every piece of my heart.

Beautiful, your passion forced its way into the door of my heart.

Beautiful, your mercy has accomplished to get a tight hold on to my heart.

Beautiful, your favor has completely taken over my heart.

Beautiful, your strength energizes the joy you placed in my heart.

Beautiful, your love has given your heart upon a cross for all the love I carry in my heart.
In Jesus name, Amen

43

Seven Times a Day

Father, you are my need, my life is nothing without you by my side.
Pour a portion of your love upon my soul. Pour the rest into my heart.
Let my heart melt into your arms.
Let it be your will to teach me to walk in the path of your commandments Father.
Seven times a day I will praise your name.

Before the sun raise I will praise you Father.
In the morning light I will praise you God.
At high noon I will praise you Father.
In the afternoon I will praise you God.
In the evening time I will praise you Father.
As the sun sets I will praise you God.
Before I lay my head down to sleep seven times a day all praise to the Lord God the Father.

Father, you are my want, my life is nothing without you keeping me from stumbling.
Let me meditate in the greatness of your mercy. Place a portion of your grace upon my soul.
Place the rest into my heart. Let my heart melt into your goodness.
Let it be your will to teach me how to walk in your way Father.
Seven times a day I will praise your name.

Before the sun raise I will praise you Father.
In the morning light I will praise you God.
When the sun is noon high I will praise you Father.
In the afternoon I will praise you God.
In the evening time I will praise you Father.
As the sun sets I will praise you God.
Before I lay my head down to sleep seven times a day all praise to the Lord God the Father.
In Jesus name, Amen

44

Through the heart of God I shall love you forever

With all of my heart I love you with all of me.
Everything that I am I love you all the time.
Through the heart of God I shall love you forever.

With all that is in me I love you with the deepest part of me.
I shall keep my heart open to you.
Never let it close for any reason.
I will just let the love flow on through me into you.
Through the heart of God I shall love you forever.

With all that I am I love you with the strongest love in me.
The breath in me cannot breathe without your life living in me.
My soul shall follow your soul beyond the end of time.
My faith has fallen into your grace forever.
I will open the door to your heart, place my love into your heart and lock the door behind me.
I live my life walking with you Jesus.
Through the heart of God I shall love you forever.
In Jesus name, Amen

45

Lord I remember the moment I died

*I kiss that drug the first time.
Now I'm seeking that first high trying to find the same feeling again.
These drugs got my life spinning my out of control. I have lost everything that I own.
Even though my families love still hold hope for me, but the love for those drug own me.
As I stand alone on that wall as those same drugs drain my soul.
All my so call friends left me dying alone. As I watch Jesus walked up and gave me a hug.
Jesus was the last face I seen looking back at me.
As I whisper God forgive me.
I think I forgot to stand up and tell all that I love goodbye.
Then I laid my head down. Closed my eyes and then I died.
With Jesus here holding my hand, Lord I remember the moment I died.

*I carried a gun, will use if need too.
Even if it's over the color I wear. At that moment I was so alone.
You just don't play with an empty gun with a lost bullet in the camber.
I lay here alone in the street. Life flashed before my eyes.
 I watch my so call family drive away with out me.
As I felt the life in me slowly drain out of my heart.
As I watch Jesus lay down by my side. Jesus was the last face I seen looking back at me.
As I whisper God forgive me.
I think I forgot to stand up and tell all that I love goodbye.
Then I lay my head down. Closed my eyes and then I died.
With Jesus here holding my hand, Lord I remember the moment I died.

*Should have gone with that feeling telling me to get out of here, I staid.
Getting in that car I wasn't suppose to sneak out.
Lied about where I was going, in the wrong place at the wrong time.
I think I meet the devil tonight just before he took my life.
As I watch Jesus stand next to me holding my hand my breath lift me.
Jesus was the last face I seen looking back at me.
As I whisper God forgive me.
I think I forgot to stand up and tell all that I love goodbye.
Then I laid my head down. Closed my eyes and than I died.
With Jesus here holding my hand, Lord I remember the moment I died.

*I went to sleep feeling weak; I was lying in my bed.

When I heard the Doc said she has lived along good life.

But by morning her precious light will burn out.

If I could open my eyes, so weak, I can feel my tears rolling down my face.

As I watch Jesus pulls up a chair and set down next to me, one hope I whisper in his ear.

Let my children say goodbye to there mama. Jesus smiled as the room filled with my family.

With tears running down all those beautiful faces.

The last strength in me raise me up, I said babies don't cry for grandmamma.

I have lived a long life and it time to go on home. As a tear roll down my face I closed my eyes.

Jesus was the last face I seen looking back at me.

As I whisper Thank you God.

Then I lay my head down. Closed my eyes and then I died.

With Jesus here holding my hand, Lord I remember the moment I died.

In Jesus name, Amen

46

I Love the Lord

When I think I am alone, before the sadness comes over me.
You touch me.
Your warmth brings a smile.
I give you all my soul.
I love the Lord.

When I just get so tired of the things that are going wrong in my life,
before I even think about giving up,
You touch me.
Your warmth brings a smile.
I give you all my heart.
I love the Lord.

When I think Lord you have left me,
before the fear comes over me,
You touch me.
Your warmth brings a smile.
I give you my entire mind.
I love the Lord.

When I think I have lost my direction,
before I even lose my way,
You touch me.
Your warmth brings a smile.
I give you my strength and all my might.
I love the Lord.
In Jesus name, Amen

47

I prayed for you

From the first moment I knew you were inside of me.
I felt you move in me, a gentle kick in my side.
I prayed for you.

From the first moment I saw your face.
I was holding you in my arm.
I felt like I could never let you go.
I prayed for you.

From the first moment I watched you take your first step.
The laughter filled the room.
Then I watched you grow and grow.
I hope Jesus will keep walking with you every moment.
I prayed for you.

From the first moment I watched you stand on your own.
Than I knew I had to let you go.
Too live your own life and find your own dreams.
I hope Jesus will keep standing by your side every moment.
I prayed for you.

I asked Jesus.
To guide every step you take.
Keep your heart open to know what is right
and to know what is wrong.
I prayed for you.

If you get lost may Jesus find you and help you to find your way.
Keep you on the lighted path.
That He will always lead you back home.
I prayed for you.

I ask Jesus to give you more good days, than bad.
Try not to get lost in the dark too many times child.
May God keep you out of harm's way?
Protect you from your enemies and yourself.
Love you unconditionally, just like me.
I prayed for you.

I hope Jesus prays for you every moment of your life, just like I still pray for you.
In Jesus name, Amen

48

Thank you Father

For having us in your kind heart, the grace you have poured out for us sinners.
Thank you, Father.

For the love you have shown us sinners, your only begotten son nailed to the cross.
Thank you, Father.

For having forgiveness in your kind heart, the mercy you have poured out for us sinners.
Thank you, Father.

For the hope you have shown us sinners, your only beloved son nailed to the cross.
Thank you, Father.

We would never be able to thank you enough.
There is not enough thank you in this world, even if we filled the universe.
We would still owe you more.
My Lord, My God,
Thank you, Father.
In Jesus name, Amen

49

Love me Lord

Some days I feel you God roaming around in me. My heart seems to stop when you pass through.
I can feel His love warm up in me.
The tears that fall from my eyes is the over flow of joy that's in my heart, my soul and my life.
God you are the blessing that dropped into my life right on time.
Looking for my soul that hides in the church you built in side of me.
Lord you are keeping my life on notice that you will always be here with me.
Everyday of my life, love me Lord.

In my dream I walk with Him so peacefully. There is where I have found the most freedom in my life.
Everyday that I awake I still feel His peace laying here with me.
God plays with my heart and His love is laughing with my soul. With Him in my life I never feel I'm alone.
Hope is always there to lead me home. Everyday of my life, love me Lord.

There is always been a humming sound coming from my heart to you God.
Wrapped in my soul singing praises too you blessing your name.
Glorifying you every moment, as your glory rejoices with my soul. He spoke to my heart, showing my soul the way to go.
As He holds my hand, He leads me down the path that brings me to the Lord.
There I found the forgiveness that freed me from my sins.
Everyday of my life, love me Lord.

You have hummed this song to me everyday of my life. I will never ever part from your heart.
Melodies that floats into my soul, with the love that belongs too you God.
Without asking God you rescued my life from sorrows wings.
Now I fly with victory, because God covered my heart with His love. God has chosen my life to be blessed with His presence.
Everyday of my life, love me Lord.

I give you my Heart will you Lord protect it from getting broken.
I give you my Soul will you Lord protect it from getting stolen.

I welcome you with open arms will you Lord forgive my life of it sins.
I welcome you with a humble heart will you Lord have passion for my soul.

I trust you with my heart will you Lord be the guide I need in my life.
I trust you with my soul will you Lord be the direction I want in my life.

You are forever in my heart. Everyday of my life, love me Lord.
In Jesus name Amen

50

Prayers of my Heart

I pray that you Lord stick by our side.
Because I know your children have lost there way.
They have showed you more wrong than you care to see.
I testify to you God that we have not always been right.
It may be that we are so busy acting holy, not seeing how much we judge one another.
You are judging everyone else instead of looking in the mirror at yourself.
We may have done more wrong than right in your eyes God.
I don't think we mean too, but we have been foolish for a very long time.
Forgive us Lord. If we are truly with God no one or nothing can stop us, from saving are own souls.
Prayers of my heart,

I pray that you my Lord don't give up on us to soon, standby our side don't let the devil win.
Hold on to our hand God don't let go even if some of us try to pull away.
Watch us every moment of our lives, be our leader as we move on through life.
Bless us everyday with your presence; keeping us strong in our spirit.
Lord you are the helping hand that we may always find our way home to you.
Prayers of my heart,

I pray that you my Lord forgive us for turning out the light in us.
Closing our ears to your voice we found ourselves lost.
I know that it is just another way we have found to become lost, forgive us Lord.
Please help us Father to turn the light in us back on.
Open our ears back up to hear your voice, I love you, with all of our hearts my Lord God.
Lord you are the Holy church that worship in me everyday of my life.
Prayers of my heart,
In Jesus name I pray A-men

Prayers of my Heart 2-51

Bless Jesus Christ

Bless Jesus Christ.

With all my Heart, Soul and Might, every night He protects me as I sleep.
Each breath that He gives me, awake me to His morning light.
Bless the Savior.

Bless Jesus Christ.

With all my Heart, Soul and Might, every time your there too comfort my life.
Each new day your breath brings me to your arms.
Bless the Savior.

Bless Jesus Christ.

With all my Heart, Soul and Might, every time you save me for myself and all the evil that steps
my way.
Each day you let me know it is your will to walk with me that I may not stumble.
Bless the Savior.
Bless Jesus Christ, for being at my side all the time.
I Jesus name, Amen

52

God is good

Each day I see God is good.
Every time I eat a meal God is good.
When I get up and walk God is good.
Every time I speak His name God is good.
Every time I pray God is good.
When I praise His name God is good.
All the time God is good.

God is good with His warm breath He awakes me.

God is good when He lays me down in His arms at night.

God is good even when He doesn't answer all our prayers,

God is good, when He sees us stumbling over our on two feet; He is there to catch us before we fall.

God is good, when we can't save ourselves He is there right on time.

God is good, with His mercy He forgives us of our sins,

God is good, when we seek, when we ask and when we knock you are always the one who answers.

God is good.
In Jesus name Amen

53

I believe in you Lord

I believe in you Lord.
Every morning I see the life that wakes me.

I believe in you Lord.
Every morning I feel your warmth that takes the chill out of the air.

I believe in you Lord.
Every high noon I see the life that walks with me to keep me on my path.

I believe in you Lord.
Every after noon I feel the strength that carries me through each day.

I believe in you Lord.
Every night you are the reason why I remember to say my prayers.

I believe in you Lord.
Every night I close my eyes as I lay safety in your arms.

I believe in you Lord My Savior, Jesus Christ.
 Amen

54

God I need you

God I love you all the time.
I wish I couldn't cry every time I hurt.
I hope that the strength in me can hold back my tears.
I have cry for this child day and night to long.
The pain always seems to find my heart.
But the tears have dried up my Lord.
God I need you now and forever.

God I love you all the time.
Each time something happen I wish my sorrow could cry.
I hope that the strength in me can hold back my tears.
I have cry for this child day and night to long.
The pain always seems to find my heart.
But the tears have dried up my Lord.
God I need you now and forever.

God I love you all the time.
I fill that all my tears have dried up inside of me.
I hope that the strength in me can hold back my tears.
I have cry for this child day and night to long.
The pain always seems to find my heart.
But the tears have dried up my Lord.
God I need you now and forever.

God I love you all the time.
Did I myself hide my tears to deep that I can't cry?
I hope that the strength in me can hold back my tears.
I have cry for this child day and night to long.
The pain always seems to find my heart.
But the tears have dried up my Lord.
If there is something is wrong in me.
Heal me with your forgiveness Lord.
Hold me; comfort me with your mercy Lord.
I hope that the strength in me can not hold back my tears no more.
God thank you for teaching me how too let go of my tears.
God I need you now and forever.
In Jesus name, Amen

55

Praise

Each morning I awake just to see your face once more.
Kiss you softly on your cheek.
Before my feet touch the floor I said a good morning prayer,
and I thank you Lord, for one more day.
I praise your name.

Each afternoon I said a prayer to you.
Then I gave bread until you are while fed.
I gave you drink to quench your thrust.
Then I touch you with my love one kiss on your forehead.
Before I finish the rest of the day,
I praise your name.

Each evening I said my prayer.
Before I lay my head down to sleep,
I touch your face.
Kiss you once again upon your cheek.
Say good night.
I praise your name.
My Lord God
In Jesus name, Amen

56

Oh how I need you Lord

Oh how I need you Lord.
Each and everyday I open my eyes; I need you Lord more and more by my side.
Oh, Lord, I need you more Jesus.

Oh how I need you Lord.
Each and every moment that I live I need you Lord more and more by my side.
Oh Lord, I need you more Jesus.

Oh how I need you Lord.
Each and every hour that I breathe I need you Lord more and more by my side.
Oh Lord, I need you more Jesus.

Oh how I need you Lord.
Each and every minute of my life I need you Lord more and more by my side.
Oh Lord, I need you more Jesus.

Oh how I need you Lord.
Each and every second that I breathe I need you Lord more and more by my side.
Oh Lord, I need you more Jesus.

Oh how I need you Lord.
Tell the end of time and beyond. I need you Lord more and more by my side.
Oh Lord, I need you more Jesus.

Oh how I need you Lord.
Each and everyday at night, before I close my eye and before I open them the next day.
I need you Lord more and more by my side.
Oh Lord, I need you more Jesus.
In Jesus name, Amen

57

I believe in you Father

If I had not took your hand Lord.
If I had not let you carry me with your will.
I would have fallen.
Then there would be no way for me to get back on my feet.
If I had not took your hand Father.
Then I would have been truly lost forever.
I believe in you, Father.

If I had a not look through your eyes Lord.
If I had not let you show me the path of your will.
I would have lost my way.
Then there would be no way for me to be found.
If I had a not looked through your eyes Father.
Then I would have been truly lost forever.
I believe in you, Father.

If I had a not lesson too your voice Lord.
If I had a not let your word guide me by your will.
I would have lived my life in fear.
Then there would be no one there to comfort my tears.
If I had a not lesson too your voice Father.
Then I would have been truly lost forever.
I believe in you, Father.

If I had not believed in you Lord.
If I had a not let your spirit move me with your will.
I would have lived with belief in me.
Then there would be no one for me to believe in me.
If I had not believed in you Father.
Then I would have been truly lost forever.
I believe in you, Father.
I Jesus name, Amen

58

Lord teach me how to pray

Lord here my plea
Lord down on my knees I bow my head to pray.
Lord Jesus hold my trimming hands pull me close to your heart were I hear each beat run though my soul.
Lord, teach me how to pray in your way.

Lord I beg of you.
Lord down on my knees I bow my head to pray.
Lord Jesus holds my hand pulls me close to your heart were I hear each breath you take run though my soul.
Lord, teach me how to pray in your way.

Lord I call on you.
Lord down on my knees I bow my head to pray.
Lord Jesus holds my shaking hands pull me close to your heart were I hear each rhythm you take run though my soul.
Lord, teach me how to pray in your way.

Lord I come to you.
Lord down on my knees I bow my head to pray.
Lord Jesus hold my hands pull me close to your heart were I hear each pocket of air you take run though my soul.
Lord, teach me how to pray in your way.
In Jesus name, Amen

59

I love you Lord

I love you Lord.
From the beginning,
for each moment of my life,
every hour,
all the time and everyday,
I love you Lord beyond the end of time.

I love the Lord.
I felt each touch you place in my heart.
I feel your voice speaking to my soul.
I feel you always there by my side.
I love you Lord forever in my heart.
In Jesus name, Amen

60

For You

Let me take your hand.
Let me hold you close.
Let me pour my love into your heart.
I will guide you every step of the way through the storm throughout your life.
I am the one, I am Jesus the Savior and I am Christ that died upon the cross for you.

Let me take your hand.
Let me hold you in my arms.
Let me pour my affection into your heart.
I will guide you every step of the way out of harm's way throughout your life.
I am the one, I am Jesus the Savior and I am Christ that died upon the cross for you.

Let me take your hand.
Let me hold you close.
Let me pour my passion into your heart.
I will guide you every step of the way down that rigid road throughout your life.
I am the one, I am Jesus the Savior and I am Christ that died upon the cross for you.

Let me take your hand.
Let me hold you in my arms.
Let me pour my life into your heart.
I will guide you every step of the way down the path that the Father has prepared for you throughout your life.
I am the one, I am Jesus the Savior and I am Christ that died upon the cross for you.
I Jesus name, Amen

61

Forever

The way your lips softly, gently kiss my heart,
You came along and filled up my empty heart with your love.
How you say I Love You,
I'm here to pick you up when you fall; together we will catch you before you touch the ground,
We are as one,
Nothing can come between us,
I love you forever,
You are the one that owns my heart God forever.

The way you hold me in your eyes,
You came along and filled up my empty heart with your love.
How you say I Love You,
I'm here to carry you for miles and miles together, beyond the end of time I am by your side tell you die,
We are as one,
Nothing can come between us,
I love you forever,
You are the one that owns my heart Jesus forever.

The way your voice pulls me into your arms,
You came along and filled up my empty heart with your love.
How you say I Love You,
I'm here to hold your hand as we walk through the storms together, down the rigid road we will walk hand and hand,
We are as one,
Nothing can come between us,
I love you forever,
You are the one that owns my heart Lord forever.
In Jesus name, Amen

62

Jesus I love your name

Jesus I just love calling your name.
Jesus I just love saying your name.
Jesus I just love hearing your name.
I love you.

Jesus I just love praising your name.
Jesus I just love blessing your name.
Jesus I just love glorifying your name.
I love you.

Jesus I just love seeing your name.
Jesus I just love rejoicing your name.
Jesus I just love singing your name.
I love you.
In Jesus name, Amen

63

My Family

God planted our family tree that grows in Him.
Together our family is grounded by the grace of our Lord the Father.
The Lord God is the strong foundation that my family is built on.
God is the milk and honey that feeds my family.
I feel all the loving prayers that my family has whisper for me to God.
To feel the warm hugs of there love drowns in me.
I am smothered by the warm forgiveness of my family.
Everyday, every step, everyplace, all the time always with open arms and you are a shoulder to lean on.
I Hope and pray that God the Father is there to keep my Family always out of harm's way.
Give them what they need to better there life in your eyes.
I always pray for my family everyday.
Because in my heart I know someone in my family has said a prayer for me.

The Lord God planted our family tree that grows in Him.
Together our family is blessed by the grace of our Lord the Father.
The Lord God is the strong foundation that my family stands on.
God is the bread and meat that feeds this family.
I feel all the loving prayers that my family has whisper for me to God.
To feel the warm hugs of there love drowns in me.
I am smothered by the warm forgiveness of my family.
Everyday, every step, everyplace, all the time always with open arms and you are a shoulder to lean on.
I Hope and pray that God the Father is there to keep my Family always out of harm's way.
Give them what they need to make it each day God you give them to breath.
I always pray for my family everyday.
Because in my heart I know someone in my family has said a prayer for me.

The Lord God planted our family tree that grows in Him.
Together our family is grounded by the love of our Lord God the Father.
The Lord God is the strong foundation that my family lives by.
God is the hunger and thirst that feeds this family.
I feel all the loving prayers that my family has whisper for me to God.
To feel the warm hugs of there love drowns in me.
I am smothered by the warm forgiveness of my family.
Everyday, every step, everyplace and all the time always with open arms and you are a shoulder to lean on.
I Hope and pray that God the Father is there to keep my Family always out of harm's way.
Give them what they need to do the right things to be always blessed by God.
I always pray for my family everyday.
Because in my heart I know someone in my family has said a prayer for me.
In Jesus name, Amen

64

Listen

I pray that Jesus prays for you to learn too listen child.
This world has too many ways that can make you trip and fall.
Hear what He has to say child.
Open up your ears and clean them out.
Listen to His voice.
Try your best to live under His protection with every step you take.
You don't want to fall and God is not there to catch you child.

I pray that Jesus prays for you to learn too listen child.
This world has too many wrong ways that will lead you in the wrong direction.
Don't roll your eyes at Him.
Don't turn your back on Him.
Don't walk away while His is still talking to you.
Let Him be the one that will come and find you when you get lost.
You don't want to fall and God is not there to catch you child.

I pray that Jesus prays for you to learn too listen child
This world has too many games that will foolishly play you for your trust.
Hear what He has to say child.
Lesson too His words.
Let Him be the one to protect you at every turn you take.
You don't want to fall and God is not there to catch you child.

I pray that Jesus prays for you to learn too listen child.
Don't let this world take you from the presence of God heart.
Don't talk back to Him, just lesson to want God has to say.
Don't mummer under your breath.
Free will is a gift from God; just don't let your life choose the wrong way.
You should not walk away while His still praying for you.
Let Him be the one that takes every step with you through your life.
You don't want to fall and God is not there to catch you child.
In Jesus name, Amen

65

Forgiveness

Forgiveness,
They may take from you forgive them.
Lie on you forgive them.
Broke you heart forgive them, but if you carry that hate.
Then they own your heart.
God don't forgive an unforgiving heart.
Let Jesus be you strength to show you how to forgive.
Be like the Lord, forgive with open arms.
Then forgive yourself.
Give it up.
Let go.
Get over it.
Let forgiveness sets your heart free.

Forgiveness,
They may steal from you forgive them.
Might not always tell the truth forgive them.
Crush you soul forgive them but if you carry that anger.
Then they own your soul.
God don't forgive an unforgiving soul.
Let Jesus be you strength to help you with forgiveness.
Be like the Lord, forgive with open arms.
Then forgive yourself.
Give it up.
Let it go.
Get over it.
Let forgiveness sets your soul free.
I Jesus name, Amen

66

Surrender

There comes a time when we must lay our lives down to God.
Be forgiven of your sins before you die.
Before the days pass you by, don't let you time run out.
Judgment day has come around.
You fine yourself stirring into God's eyes and find them closed to you.
Yes, I surrender my life to you my Lord.
Yes, I surrender all of me.
God how did you save my life yesterday.
Yes, I surrender to you Father.

There come a time when we must stop playing with God.
Be forgiven of all those sins before life comes to an end.
Remember to set your clock you don't want to miss the coming of the Lord.
Stop sleeping your days away when God is waiting on you.
Judgment day has come around.
You don't want to wakeup watching God wave goodbye.
Yes, I surrender my life to you my Lord.
Yes, I surrender all of me.
God I ask you to save my life once again today.
Yes, I surrender to you.

It's time to open our eyes too see were we have carried our lives without God.
Stand up ask God for forgiveness before you pass on to the other side.
Lost in our own guilty ways, hoping God fines us real soon before it gets too dark.
You don't want to be lost on this path and God want be there to lead you home.
Judgment day comes calling
I pray that God gives us a push in the right direction.
Yes, I surrender my life to you my Lord.
Yes, I surrender all of me.
God I hope you are there to save my life tomorrow.
Yes, I surrender to you.

Be your own hero and save yourself for God,
and always lesson you just might here God walk up and set down next to you.
Surrender yourself.
In Jesus name, Amen

67

My Hero is God

There are times when I get lost.
My hero is always there to find me.
My hero is God.
When I am sad, my hero brings laugher to my soul.
My hero is God.

There are times when I get lonely.
My hero is always there to comfort me.
My hero is God.
When I am in deep sorrow, my hero brings joy to my heart.
My hero is God.

There are times when I stumble.
My hero is always there to catch me.
My hero is God.
When I am in tears, my hero brings a smile to my soul.
My hero is God.

There are times when I struggle with life.
My hero is always there to save me.
My hero is God.
When I am in need of God, my hero brings open arms to my heart.
My hero is God.
In Jesus name, Amen

68

I need my Hero

I will never let my heart walk away for loving you my Lord.
I need my hero to be with me everyday in my life.

I will never let my heart fail from loving you my Lord.
I need my hero to be the guide in my life.

I will never let my heart stop loving you my Lord.
I need my hero to be the light in my life.

I will never let my heart give upon loving you my Lord.
I need my hero to be the will in my life.

I will never let my heart quit loving you my Lord.
I need my hero to be the breath in my life.

I will never let my heart forget about loving you my Lord.
I need my hero to be always apart of my life.

I will never let my heart turn off from loving you my Lord.
I need my hero to be the leader in my life.

I will never let my heart run from loving you my Lord.
I need my hero to be the Savior in my life.
In Jesus name, Amen

69

Jesus I believe in you

Jesus I believe in you.
Each morning I awake from my sleep.
Too see your smile breathe live in me.
Jesus I thank you for one more day.
I hope I walk this journey looking through the eyes of my Lord Jesus Christ.
That you will guide me down the right path,
I pray in the name of Jesus.
That it be Gods will to direct my life.
Because I rather live my life believing in Jesus Christ our Savior,
Then die not believing in you Father.
Rather live my life through Jesus' eyes.
Than die just to hear you say you don't know me.
Jesus I believe in you.

Jesus I believe in you.
Each morning I awake from my sleep
To see the smile that beats in my heart.
Jesus I thank you for one more day.
I hope I walk this road looking through the eyes of my Lord Jesus Christ.
That you may give me strength to keep my feet for slipping,
I pray in the name of Jesus.
That it be Gods will to catch me before I fall.
Because I rather live my life believing in Jesus Christ our Savior,
Then die not believing in you Father.
Rather live my life through Jesus' eyes.
Than die just to hear you say you don't know me.
Jesus I believe in you.

Jesus I believe in you.
Each morning I awake from my sleep.
To see the smile that woke my soul.
Jesus I thank you for one more day.
I hope I walk this life looking through the eyes of my Lord Jesus Christ.
That you may have mercy too keep my steps out of harm's way,
I pray in the name of Jesus.
That it be Gods will to carry me though it all.
Because I rather live my life believing in Jesus Christ our Savior,
Then die not believing in you Father.
Rather live my life through Jesus eyes.
Than die just to hear you say you don't know me.
Jesus I believe in you.
In Jesus name, Amen

70

No joy without you Jesus

You are my joy that I must breathe.
Everyday, every way in my life, without you Jesus I surely will lose my way in my life.

There will be no joy in my life without you Lord.

There will be no joy in my heart without you Jesus.

There will be no joy in my soul without you Savior.

There only will be sorrow from miss you my Lord Jesus.

You are my joy that I must feel running through me.
Everyday, every way in my life, without you Jesus I surely will stumble throughout my life.

There will be no joy in my smile without you Lord.

There will be no joy in my laughter without you Jesus.

There will be no joy in my eyes without you Savior.

There only will be tears from miss you my Lord Jesus.
In Jesus name, Amen

71

I Love you, God

I Love you Father.
Even though I may have strayed away sometimes,
but my love for you Lord will never fade away from my heart.
I Love you God.

I Love you Father.
Even though I may have lost my way sometimes,
but my love for you Lord will never lose its way from my heart.
I Love you God.

I Love you Father.
Even though I may have let go of your hand sometimes,
but my love for you Lord will never let go of you in my heart.
I Love you God.

I Love you Father.
Even though I may have not listened sometimes,
but my love for you Lord will never stop listening to your voice in my heart
I Love you God.

I Love you Father.
Even though I may have not call on you sometimes,
but my love for you Lord will never forget about you in my heart.
I Love you God
In Jesus name, Amen

72

Lovely Lord

Lovely Lord, I believe in the love of the Father the Son and the Holy Ghost.
So let your love flow through my soul.

Lovely Lord, I trust in the love of the Father, the Son and the Holy Ghost.
So let your love fill my heart.

Lovely Lord, I give thanks for the love of the Father, the Son and the Holy Ghost.
So let your love grow always in me.

Lovely Lord, I give praise for the love of the Father, the Son and the Holy Ghost.
So let your love move around forever in me.

Lovely Lord, I give my life for the love of the Father, the Son and the Holy Ghost.
So let your love, live every moment in me.
In Jesus name, Amen

73

Come meet the Father, the Son and the Holy Ghost

Come.
Set a while.
Feed your soul.
Quench your thirsty heart.
Get to know them.
Tell them all your troubles.
Let them be the answer to your life.
Come meet the Father, the Son and the Holy Ghost.

Come.
Set a while.
Feed your soul.
Quench your thirsty heart.
Get to know them.
Tell them all your problems.
Let them open the door to your heart.
Come meet the Father, the Son and the Holy Ghost.

Come.
Set a while.
Feed your soul.
Quench your thirsty heart.
Get to know them.
Tell them all about how your burdens weight your life down.
Let them give you peace in your soul.
Come meet the Father, the Son and the Holy Ghost.

Come.
Set a while.
Feed your soul
Quench your thirsty heart.
Get to know them.
Let them give you hope to heal the pain in your soul.
Let them show you what love really feels like in your heart.
Let them show you what it is like to have them guide your life.
Come meet the Father, the Son and the Holy Ghost.
In Jesus name, Amen

74

I sing a song to thank my Lord God

I sing a song to thank my Lord God, for loving me with all His heart.
I sing a song to thank my Lord God, for being the life in my heart.
I sing a song to thank my Father, for giving us His only begotten joy, our Lord Jesus Christ.
Jesus is a sacrifice that fell out of Gods heart, long ago.
I sing a song to thank my Lord Jesus, for giving His life for the forgiveness of our sins.

Jesus has opened His heart and His love fell upon the cross long ago.
Today His blood still runs in every heart that believes in Him.
Jesus' love has never stop living in me. What a joy He is to breathe everyday.

O how beautiful is the Lamb of God.
O how beautiful is the Life of God.
O how beautiful is the Light of God.
O how beautiful is the Word of God.

I sing a song to thank my Lord God, for always being the life that breathes in my heart.
I sing a song to thank my Lord Jesus, for carrying me and always there by my side to comfort me.
I sing a song to thank my Father, for keeping faith, hope, and love growing in me.
I sing a song to thank the Father and the Lord Jesus.
Jesus is an offing that was poured out of Gods heart, long ago.
For being there when I am in need of him keeping me out of harm's way.

Jesus has a leak in His heart and His love drops upon the cross, long ago.
His life still runs in every heart that believes in His love.
Jesus' life has never stop living in me. What a joy He is to breathe everyday.

O how beautiful is the Lamb of God.
O how beautiful is the Life of God.
O how beautiful is the Light of God.
O how beautiful is the Word of God.

I sing a song to thank my Lord God for the precious gift you gave our hearts and let breathe in our lives.
In Jesus name, Amen

75

How do you know that you love the Father, the Son and the Holy Ghost?

When someone enters into your heart uninvited your body shakes.
Touch you more than you have ever known in your life.
How do you know that you love the Father, the Son and the Holy Ghost?

He who woke up something more than the love in me,
He who found something more than the need in me,
He who brought out something more than I thought I had in me.
He who looked into something deeper than I knew was in me.

I felt your touch heal my soul.
I felt your joy jump around in my heart.
I felt your truth fill my mind.
I heard the gentle warmth of your voices run through my heart, my soul and my mind.
Saying your the Lord the Almighty One.

He who put something more than I want in me,
He who placed something more than Himself in me,
He who took my heart, my soul and my mind lift something stronger than the life in me.
He who entered something more than His love in me,

How do you know that you love the Father, the Son and the Holy Ghost?
When you give all your heart, soul and mind to the Lord the Almighty One forever.
In Jesus name Amen

76

Jesus

Though, I have fallen down.
I have gotten up and yes I have dust myself off.
Jesus with you by my side, I hold my head up high because of you.
I have stumble and caught myself slipping.
I turned lift when I should have turned right.
Jesus with you by my side, I can hold my head up high because of you.
I will never ever stop loving you Jesus.

Sometimes I have straddled that fence.
Thinking I may find something better on the other side.
I guest we sometime get blind.
Leaving behind are family and friends.
Lost on a road that never ends.
Found by the love that never gives up on me.
Jesus with you by my side, I can hold my head up high because of you.
I will never ever stop loving you Jesus.
In Jesus name, Amen

77

God has blessed me

Thank you Lord.

God has blessed me with a special gift of His love that He placed inside of me.

God has blessed me with his hope that grows in me.

God has blessed me with a surprise kiss that woke in me.

God has blessed me with a wish that come truth in me.

God has blessed me with joy that lives in me.

God has blessed me with His touch that moves all around in me.

God has blessed me with life that breathes in me.

God has blessed me with the church he as built in me.

You are the kingdom of love, Thank you Lord God.
In Jesus name, Amen

78

God's flower grows in me

The moment I learn to trust my Lord Jesus.
He turn the light back on in side my soul.
The flower that God planted in me start to grow.
The moment I learn to love my Lord Jesus.

The more I read about Him.
The more I hear about Him.
The more I talk about Him.
His word feeds the seed that God planted in me.
God's flower grows in me.

The more I learn about my Lord Jesus Christ.
The more the flower grow that God planted in me.
Let my Soul grow by the word of God.
Let my Heart grow by the blood of Jesus.
God's flower grows in me.

The moment I learn to believe in my Lord Jesus.
He turn the life back on in side my heart.
The flower that God planted in me start to grow.
The moment I learn to live in the Lord Jesus.

The more I read about Him.
The more I hear about Him.
The more I talk about Him.
His word brings joyful tears that watered the flower that God planted in me.
God's flower grows in me.

The more I learn about my Lord Jesus Christ.
The more the flower grow that God planted in me.
Let my Soul grow by the word of God.
Let my Heart grow by the blood of Jesus.
God's flower grows in me.
In Jesus name, Amen

79

A Family tree that is only feed by God

I want my family tree to be grown by the love, faith, hope, and believing in the Lord God the Father.

Our family tree is only fed by God, Jesus Christ and the Holy Spirit.

Let this family be raised by the word of God.

Let this family tree breath, eat, drink and live in the light of God.

We were fed by the mercy of our Lord Jesus.

May this family be bonded by the love, trust, forgiveness and the will of the Father?

Let this tree be planted and fed by the love that God has showed on this family for generation to generation,

we shell walk in the light of God.

Wait on the Lord for He is coming any day, any time and any place praises His name.

God brought this family together filled with the Holy Spirit as we are walking in the glory of God.

God loves us in every way.

We have learned everything about life, love, hope and believing how to keep the faith of God growing in us.

Family is the loved ones that you will have too forgiven more than anyone in this world.

Living in His understanding and grace of God, breathe in His glory and forgive His wondering child.

Our generation has stamped the love of God across their hearts forever.

We truly need God in are lives all the time, everyplace, every turn and every moment.

We breathe and live by the word of God the Father, because He has fed us with His knowledge and wisdom he placed in us to grow throughout our life.

We will stand fast living in His faith.

If we could live, love, see and feel through God then our lives would be fulfilled.

The faith, the forgiveness, the understanding and the love will only grow stronger in our hearts with God at our side, forever.

In Jesus name, Amen

80

My little Angel

Jesus has set an angel at your right hand just to hold you as you walk throughout your life.
My little angel, only Jesus knows where life is going to carry you before you take your first steps.
Jesus has set an angel at your lift hand too keep the devil out your ear.
My little angel, only Jesus knows what road you are going to take before you take that turn.
Jesus has set an angel before you too keep you on the right path
My little angel, only Jesus knows when you will fall and how long you will crawl before you are back on your feet.
Jesus has set an angel behind you too protect you and someone to keep the devil of your back.
My little angel, only Jesus knows when you will get lost and how long you will be wondering around before you will be found.

Jesus has placed His protection all around your young heart.
My little angel, only Jesus knows your young heart.
Were ever you go you will always be safe from harm.
My little angel, only Jesus knows your young soul.
Each day He will feed your little soul with His words.
My little angel, only Jesus knows your young mind.
Every moment He will save you from yourself by His will.
My little angel, only Jesus knows your young needs.

An angel sets at your right ready to walk with you on this journey through your young life.
My little angel, only Jesus knows the steps in your life.
An angel sets at your lift ready to catch you before you fall off your path, in your young life.
My little angel, only Jesus knows the path in your life.
An angel sets before you ready to guide you through your young life.
My little angel, only Jesus knows how to guide your life.
An angel sets behind you ready to direct your young life with the will of God.
My little angel, only Jesus knows how to direct your young life.

My little angel just follows, Jesus
In Jesus name, Amen

81

I believe I hope God stole my heart

I believe I hope God stole my heart.
Each time I looked I from my heart, I found it drowning in His love.
Because he wake's up my heart every time I think of Him I smile.
Tears fall from my eyes, just because you are God.

I believe I hope God stole my heart.
Every time I searched for my heart I found it curled up in His arms.
Because he breathes in my heart every time I feel Him I cry.
Tears fall from my eyes, just because you are God.

I believe I hope God stole my heart.
Each time I looked I from my heart, I found my heart hid behind God.
Because he touches my heart every time I feel him move in me.
Tears fall from my eyes, just because you are God.

I believe I hope God stole my heart.
Every time I searched for my heart I found it sleeping in His joy.
Because he lit up my heart every time I think of Him my heart jumps for joy.
Tears fall from my eyes, just because you are God.

I believe I hope God stole my heart.
Each time I looked I from my heart, I found it walking with God.
Because he is the comfort every time I need him to hold me he just pull me lie into his arms.
Tears fall from my eyes, just because you are God.

I believe I hope God stole my heart.
Every time I searched for my heart I found my heart setting in His Glory.
Because he is the flame that burns in my heart every time I remember that His life lives in me.
Tears fall from my eyes, just because you are God.

I believe I hope God stole my heart.
Each time I looked I from my heart, I found it locked away forever in His heart.
Because his love runs around in my heart every time I pray, I feel and I know your peace is in me.
Tears fall from my eyes, just because you are God.
In Jesus name, Amen

82

Lord we may be young

Lord we may be young.
But we give you our hearts forever.
Some may say that we are too young to love you Jesus.
But Lord who can standup and say that a young heart can't love the Lord.
And who Lord knows this young heart better than you Jesus.
Will we not be judged by the love we have for you or by our young age.
Because we may not have walked down the roads, that most have traveled.
And we may be too young to have any burden to carry.
But that don't mean we don't need Jesus to guide us by His will.

If you are raised to always praise the Lord with all your heart.
Would you say then I love Jesus?
If you are taught to always praise the Lord with all your soul.
Would you say then I love Jesus?
If you are raised to know the Father that gave His only begotten son.
Would you say then I love Jesus?

Lord we may be young.
But we give you our souls forever.
Some may say that we are too young to love you Jesus.
But Lord who can testify and say that a young soul can't love the Lord.
And who Lord knows this young soul better than you Jesus.
Will we not be judged by the love we have for you Jesus, or by our young age.
Because we may not have walked down the path, that most have journeyed.
And we may be too young to have any heavy loads to carry.
But that don't mean we don't need Jesus to direct us by His will.

If you are raised to always praise the Lord with all your heart.
Would you say then I love Jesus?
If you are taught to always praise the Lord with all your soul.
Would you say then I love Jesus?
If you are raised to know the Father that gave His only begotten son.
Would you say then I love Jesus?
Lord we may be young, but our hearts our wide open to receive your love.
We lay down our soul at your feet, my Lord,
You are never too young to give Jesus your Heart and God your soul.
In Jesus name, Amen

83

God has all the answers

He guides my heart.
Every turn I take you are there with all the answers.
He already knows the questions in my heart.
God has all the answers.

He directs my life.
Everyplace I went you were there with all the answers.
You read all the questions on my mind.
God has all the answers.

He leads my soul.
Every step I took you was there with all the answers.
You knew the questions that hunt my soul.
God has all the answers.
I Jesus name, Amen

84

God is here now and it is time to love

Love rejoices when God has something to do with your life.
You find in your life nothing works without love.
Love must start your life.
Move you down that road without sorrow.
Love must end your life dying in God arms.
Keep the door open to your heart.
Don't let a bump in the road close your heart up.
God is here now and it is time to love.

Give up all the suffering in your heart.
God is here now and it is time to love.
You cannot hide behind your broken heart.
God is here now and it is time to love.

Failure comes when you doubt the love God has for your life.
You find in your life nothing works without love.
Love must start your life.
Move you down that path without resentment.
Love must end your life dying in God hands.
Keep the light on in your heart.
Don't let the warmth in your heart turn cold.
God is here now and it is time to love.

Don't shut that door with doubt in your heart.
God is here now and it is time to love.
Stop being selfish covering up your heart.
God is here now and it is time to love.

Keep your heart open, keep your mind free and let your life find love.
God is here now and it is time to love.
In Jesus name, Amen

85

Proud

I'm so proud that I believe you lived.

I'm so proud that you are apart of me.

I'm so proud that I give you my soul.

I'm so proud that you are what I need.

I'm so proud that you have touched my heart and every part of me in this life.

I'm so proud of you God for given us your only begotten son, Jesus Christ.

I'm so proud of you Jesus for given your beautiful life for the forgiveness of our sins.

I'm so proud of loving you God with my hold heart even when there are some trying to pull me out of your arms.

I'm so proud that I believe in you God even when some say you are not real.

I'm so proud that you God keep me in your prayers.

I'm so proud that I gave you all my love Jesus.

I'm so proud that I walk with you everyday of my life my Lord.

I'm so proud to love you God.
In Jesus name, Amen

86

Would God forgive his child?

*If a child that has done lied to many times. He said he love the Father.
Would you believe him? Would God forgive His child?
Tell me can you see into his heart just like the Lord.
Are do you believe only God can tell you what's in someone heart.
Would God forgive His child, I say yes.
*If she walks the streets, using all that she is too pay her bills.
She said she loves the Father, would you believe her?
Would God forgive His child? Tell me can you see into her heart just like the Lord.
Are do you believe only God can tell you what's in someone heart.
Would God forgive His child, I say yes.
*If he has killed and his heart remain still.
He said he loves the Father, would you believe him?
Would God forgive His child? Tell me can you see into his heart just like the Lord.
Are do you believe only God can tell you what's in someone heart.
Would God forgive His child, I say yes.
*If she has stolen everything you own.
She said she loves the Father, would you believe her?
Would God forgive His child? Tell me can you see into her heart just like the Lord.
Are do you believe only God can tell you what's in someone heart.
Would God forgive His child, I say yes.
*If a child that has cost you too much.
He or she said they love the Father, would you believe them?
Would God forgive His child? Tell me can you see into there heart just like the Lord.
Are do you believe only God can tell you what's in someone heart.
Would God forgive His child, I say yes.
*If a father that cheats and lies around.
He said he loves the Father, would you believe him?
Would God forgive His child? Tell me can you see into his heart just like the Lord.
Are do you believe; only God can tell you what's in someone heart.
Would God forgive His child, I say yes,
*If a mother that only think of drugs and forgets her child.
She said she loves the Father, would you believe her?
Would God forgive His child? Tell me can you see into her heart just like the Lord.
Are do you believe only God can tell you what's in someone heart.
Would God forgive His child, I say yes.
*If they all are down on there knees praying for forgiveness.
They said they love the Father, would you believe them?
Would God forgive His children sins? Tell me can you see into their heart just like the Lord.
Are do you believe only God can tell you what's in someone heart.
Would God forgive His child, I say yes.
In Jesus name, Amen

87

Victory

There are only three steps to Victory, the Father, the Son and the Holy Ghost.

The first step is the Father.
You are my merciful Master.
The hand that leads my life with ever step in the name of His will.
You guide my heart into your arms Father.
You are the kingdom that grows in my soul.
Father you are my Victory.

The second step is the Son.
You are the life that breathes in me from the beginning of my life.
You are the life that dead upon a cross for my sins.
My Savior Jesus Christ you have directed my love into your heart.
You are the kingdom that grows in my soul.
Jesus Christ you are my Victory.

The third step is the Holy Ghost.
You are the teacher that taught me how to walk in God's light.
You are the Spirit that lit up the darkness in my life.
The Holy Ghost you are the light that helps me find my direction into Gods heart.
You are the kingdom that grows in my soul.
Holy Ghost you are my Victory.
In Jesus name, Amen

88

Wrap your love around me Lord

Jesus, thank you.
Lord for wrapping your gentle arms around my heart.
You breathe in your love wakening up my soul.
He Squeezed His love into my heart.
So wrap your love around my life.
Hold me close to you soul.
I want to be here in your arms forever.
Wrap your love around me Lord Jesus Christ.

Jesus, thank you.
Lord for wrapping your gentle arms around my soul.
You breathe in your love wakening up my heart.
He Squeezed His love into my soul.
So wrap your love around my love let our love grow together forever.
So wrap your soul around my soul let them grow forever together.
Hold me closed let my love always follow you wherever you may go.
Hold me closed let my soul always hold on to your hand.
Wrap your love around me Lord Jesus, thank you.
In Jesus name, Amen

89

Feel the Power of Love

Have you ever felt something so soft and kind?
He has a force that blesses everything inside of you.
God runs through your soul into your heart.
Feel the power of love.

Have you ever felt something so amazing?
That grows the joy inside of you.
God rush through your soul into your heart.
Feel the power of love.

Have you ever felt something so precious and real?
That feeds the love that breathes inside of you.
God moves through your soul into your heart.
Feel the power of love.

Have you ever felt something so warm and strong?
That moves around gently inside of you
God ran through your soul into your heart.
Feel the power of love.

Have you ever felt something so sweet and powerful?
That heals all the tears and pain inside of you.
God races through your soul into your heart.
Feel the power of love.
In Jesus name, Amen

90

Be just a breath away

There's nothing in my life that's more important than you God.
Your love drowns in my heart over flows into my soul.
So when I call on your name oh Lord.
In a blink of an eye be just a breath away.

There's always a want, a need for you to be in my life God.
Your love is lost in my heart.
I found you wondering in my soul.
So when I call on your name oh Lord.
In a blink of an eye be just a breath away.

There's no time I'm willing to leave your side or give you up in my life God.
Your love took over my heart stole my soul.
So when I call on your name oh Lord.
In a blink of an eye be just a breath away.

There's no where in my life I rather be without you or in a place where I can't find you God.
Your love has blessed my heart.
Jump for joy in my soul.
So when I call on your name oh Lord.
In a blink of an eye be just a breath away.
In Jesus name, Amen

91

Presence of the Lord

I set in the presence of the Lord.
I feel His sweetness moving around in my soul.
I welcome His kindness as He pours it into my heart.
I set in the presence of His love.

I set in this house that God built within my soul.
I set in this house with wall made from God's love.
As I set here I can feel His life move through me.
I set in the presence of God the Father.

I set in the presence of the Lord.
I feel His gentleness moving around in my soul.
I welcome His joyfulness as He pours it into my heart
I set in the presence of His love.

I set in this house that God built within my soul.
I set in this house with wall made from God's grace.
As I set here I can feel His light move through me.
I set in the presence of the Lord Jesus Christ.

I sct in the presence of the Lord.
I feel His greatness moving around in my soul.
I welcome His preciousness as He pours it into my heart.
I set in the presence of His love.

I set in this house that God built within my soul.
I set in this house with wall made from God's glory.
As I set here I can feel His energy move through me.
I set in the presence of the God the Father.

I set in the presence of the Lord.
I feel His peacefulness moving around in my soul.
I welcome His goodness as He pours it into my heart.
I set in the presence of His love.

I set in this house that God built within my soul.
I set in this house with wall made from God's forgiveness.
As I set here I can feel His power move through me.
I set in the presence of the Lord Jesus Christ.

I am truly blessed.
How God has always been here setting with me.
I love walking in your peace, I love standing in His joy.
I love setting in the presence of the Lord.
In Jesus name, Amen

92

I will love you

I will love you every moment that I breathe.
You are the breath that grows in me.
God you are the love that feeds the needs in my soul.
Your love is the water that quenches my thirst in my heart.
I inhale your love every moment of my life, Lord.
I exhale all my sins for your forgiveness my Lord.
I thank you for letting your love lay down in me.

I will love you every minute that I breathe.
You are the breath that breathes in me.
God you are the joy that feeds the needs in my soul.
Your joy is the water that quenches my thirst in my heart.
I inhale your joy every minute of my life, Lord.
I exhale all my sins for your forgiveness my Lord.
I thank you for letting your joy walk hand and hand with me.

I will love you every second that I breathe.
You are the breath that grew up in me.
God you are the word that feeds the needs in my soul.
Your word is the water that quenches my thirst in my heart.
I inhale your word every second of my life, Lord.
I exhale all my sins for your forgiveness my Lord.
I thank you for letting your word teach me your song that sings in me.
In Jesus name, Amen

93

Come dance with me my Lord

Take my hand my Lord Jesus Christ.
Let your love dance across my heart.
With your love melting into my soul every moment I'm in your arms.
Come dance with me my Lord.

Take my hand my Lord Jesus Christ.
Let your love move across my heart.
With your love draining into my soul every moment I'm in your arms.
Take my hand my Lord Jesus Christ.
Let every step of your love walk across my heart.
With your love running into my soul every moment I'm in your arms.
Come dance with me my Lord.

Take my hand my Lord Jesus Christ.
Let your love twist across my heart.
With your love twirling around in side my soul every moment I'm in your arms.
Take my hand my Lord Jesus Christ.
Let every step of your love walk across my heart.
With your love running into my soul every moment I'm in your arms
Come dance with me my Lord.

Take my hand my Lord Jesus Christ.
Let the love of you grow across my heart.
With your love energize in my soul every moment I'm in your arms.
Take my hand my Lord Jesus Christ.
Let every step of your love walk across my heart.
With your love running into my soul every moment I'm in your arms.
Come dance with me my Lord.
In Jesus name, Amen

94

Let's dance with the Spirit of God

Clap your hands.
The Spirit of God has entered to join us in this morning worship.
Stand on your feet.
The Spirit of God is dance around the room.
His Spirit is here to teach us how to dance in His way.
How too move in His Spirit with in our lives. His love smoothers us every moment.
As He dance into our hearts, our souls and our mind. Then He starts all over again.
With a smile, through His eyes I watch the Spirit of God dance down that road with our life in His arms.
Let's dance with the Spirit of God.

Raise your hands.
The Spirit of God has moved into join us in this morning worship.
Stand on your feet.
The Spirit of God is dancing around our lives.
He's Spirit is here to show us how to dance in His light.
How to walk in His Spirit within our lives,
He drowns us with His love. As He dance into our heart, our soul and our mind. Then He starts all over again.
With a smile, through His eyes I watch the Spirit of God dance down that path with our life in His hands.
Let's dance with the Spirit of God.
In Jesus name, Amen

95

Come walk with me Lord

Come walk with me Lord.
I will hold your hand wherever you may take me I'll go.

I have been led by His will.
I was dry and you give me drink.
Come walk with me Lord.

I have been fed with thus sweet fruit.
The glory of your waters has quenched my soul.
Come walk with me Lord.

I have been fed with Thus Holy bread.
I am so thirsty for your voice to speak to me.
Come walk with me Lord.

But Lord I am still hungry for your words to embrace me.
Everyday, every night nothing fills me up when it comes to your word.
Come walk with me Lord.

Your voice rocks my soul.
When you speak my heart skips a beat.
Come walk with me Lord.

The joy you bring me oh how I love you with all of me.
Take my hand, direct my feet and guide my life with your will.
Come walk with me Lord.
In Jesus name, Amen

96

To God

I Love you God every minute of the day and in the night my dreams sing a soft melody to you.
I love you Lord. You are my number one friend. You are the number one heart. You are the number one soul.
You are the number one Father. I love you God my number one love.

We need to wake up knowing that God will save us form ourselves.
Keep our enemy out of our lives. He will be our every step to protect us from harm's way.
In every moment of our lives we also need to know that God loves us unconditionally.
Understanding, forgiveness can make the heart strong.
He is the key that opens the wisdom that's lock in our souls.
I praise, I bless and I give all glory to God the Father in Jesus name Amen.

Pray for it and leave it alone, God heard it the first time.
Lit Him think about it, if it is for you then God will give it to you and if not then you want receive it.
Be happy let God be your direction in your life.

The devil is always whispering in your ear you just got to be strong enough to ignore Him.
In life you see how some ignore and some lesson, but those that lesson lose there way.
Because the devil is for no one best interest only His own. It is hard to love some one you never see or seen.
Fill the warmth of God's touch every time He places His hand upon you. Your body shacks with thankfulness.
I will be one of those who believe in God with my hold heart before I died.
Bless it is the Father and all that He carries with Him in His grace.

God is the strength of the family. Those that do not lesson surely will loss their way early in life.
Their family and their friends no one could tell them anything.
They just know it all letting sorrow take over there lives.
Did they leave our Lord back on that road?
Sometimes we must turn around to find are way home. At that moment will they remember God?
Will they lay there life down at your feet Lord.
God they know in their hearts that you will always be there waiting with open arms at the end of sorrows road.

I forgot to pray and I forgot to ask God to walk with me all the way.

I did not praise your name when I should have. I was having too must fun, parting too hard and the music was too loud.

I just did not hear you call my name. Then I felt you wondering around in me.

Now it times to give you Lord my life. So I looked in my soul and I found your foot steps walking into my heart.

There I found God just wanting to love me and wanting to hold me. I just want you God to walk with me in my life.

In Jesus name, Amen

97

My precious Lord, I love you

Sometimes we get lost.
I have walked this road along time now.
I have served my time with this world.
I have lied; I have sin, now it is time to stop playing.
It is time for my life to find God and lay down all of me at His feet.
God you can do as you will with my life because now it belongs to you.
My precious Lord, I love you.

I know God, you took my heart.
Every moment I feel Him in my life.
I just cry for no reason and my tears fall free because I'm so happy.
Too be here in the presence of the Lord.
God swept out the sins in my heart and than He set up His love in me.
My precious Lord, I love you.

I know God stole my soul.
Because every time I seek Him I find Him in my life.
I just smile for no reason and peace runs through my soul.
Filling my heart with more love than my heart can hold.
God has my life wondering around in a daze I am under His spell of love.
My precious Lord, I love you.

I know God has runway with my heart.
I heard Him laughing just before the door closed behind Him.
Then I felt His joy melting into my soul.
My life disappears into the arms of His heart.
I have found my new beginning in God.
God has built me a home in His heart made out of His love.
My precious Lord, I love you.
In Jesus name, Amen

98

Every drop of my love belong to you Jesus

Every drop of my love belongs to you Jesus.
Will you completely give me your love Jesus?
I will completely give you my heart.

Every drip of my love I give to you Jesus.
Will you entirely give me your love Jesus?
I will entirely give you my soul.

Every quantity of my love I give to you Jesus.
Will you endlessly give me your love Jesus?
I will endlessly give you my heart.

Every piece of my love I give to you Jesus.
Will you eternally give me your love Jesus?
I will eternally give you my soul.
Every drop of my love belongs to you Jesus.
In Jesus name, Amen

99

God is watching over you

Mama said child hold your head up.
Before you trap and fall.
You got to see were you are going.
You don't want to step on the wrong path.
Jesus eyes are wide open to you.
He is there to walk you thought all things.
God is watching over you.

Can you feel His stare upon you?
Every move you take His eyes follow you.
Everyday, everyplace and every moment He watches over you.
Jesus has His eyes always locked on you.
Too keep you safe from finding yourself on the wrong road.
God is watching over you.

Mama said child hold your head up.
Before you fall over your on two feet look up, look down and look around.
You got to see were your steps are taking you.
Stop looking for help in the wrong places.
Jesus is here to show you the way.
Stop acting like this is a game.
God is watching over you.

Every moment His eyes position themselves upon you.
Every way, everywhere and every minute He watches over you.
Jesus has His eyes always fixed on you.
To keep you out of harm's way every step of your life.
God is watching over you.
In Jesus name, Amen

100

God's door is never locked

Mama said God's Door is never locked.
His arms are always open wide.
He's the one, who dries the rain storm that falls from your eyes.
When darkness has fallen upon your heart He's your light.
Every moment He's there by your side to hold you tight.
He knows how many days you have been lost.
How many times He has found you.
He can count every smile when things were going good.
How many frowns when things were going bad.
All the hurt, the suffering you had to carry through your life.
Happiness in your heart for all the days you praised God.
But did you know that God was there too.
Standing there holding your hand as He walked by your side.
All that joy from your laugher thanks God.
When life has taken everything or so mush from you.
You must open your eye and see Him that stands before you.
If you loss some of your life on your journey, God will give it all back.
You have given him the key to your heart where you have hidden your soul.
Mama said it's time to pray, and let God be the one to breathe that life back into you always.
God's door is never locked.
In Jesus name, Amen

101

God has open my eyes to the world

God has opened my eyes to the world.
It's looking mighty ugly.
Not so pretty.
Just being mean, to hate for no reason.
Very scary too be so unhappy.
No faith, no understanding and no forgiveness.
Self destruction is running around trying to start trouble.
Giving up on your dreams and giving up on yourself.
Given up on your life, suicide become a pass time.
Letting drugs rule over your soul.
Like a high you never come down.
Have too much fun stepping on everyone that gets in your way.
Your guilty, you judged and the righteous has to prove there innocents.
A lie is the truth and the truth is a lie.
Money means more then someone's life.
It's like everyone is running in and out the door, that never close, that never locks.
We become lost in this worldly trap.
Like a rat the devil has caught.
You just one more lost child.
I hope you tried to find the light that brings you back to God.
I pray that God open your eyes to the world, child.

My eyes have seen the world come in and out the door.
Some came with God and lift alone.
Some came alone and lift with God.
When we look at the world through our owe eyes we seem to get lost into the worldly things.
Distracted by those who has played with God for many years?
Pray that God give you a blessing to see through his eyes.
Then you will know the beauty and the ugliness that has walked across this earth.
Through the eyes of God you shell see nothing but the truth.
Let God be your source of life He is waiting for you to just say yes.
Lord saves me from myself, harm's way and everyone else that hates me.
Keep my life in your hands, day and night.
God has opened my eyes to the worldly things.
Through all the ugliness I have found the good in me, it's you God.
In Jesus name, Amen

102

God loves you

Each morning you my Lord awake me with your warm embrace.
Before I open my eyes I seem to get a glimpse of your face.
That is what makes my day a good day.
Your strength touches me and I breathe one more day.
I lay there in my bed.
Then I say a prayer that everyday God be the one to plan my day.
Keep me safe out of harm's way.
That God take every step with all my loved ones, my enemies and me.
God be are protector every minute of the day, before my feet touch the floor.
I hope all my prayers are whispered in God's ears.
I pray that Jesus move a little closer to me.
God never lets my tear clover up my smile.
I let Jesus dry up all the sins that try to drown me in my life.
The greatness love of all is God He has touched my heart with His love in so many ways.
Listen; hear the Holy Ghost speak the truth.
God loves you.

I don't want to travel no more down these dark roads.
I'm tried of being lost on this crooked path.
I pray that God hold out His hand and lead me home.
That Jesus pulls me back into the light again.
My destiny is to be controlled by God.
My soul desire is to get lost in the heart of Jesus.
I hope God take time to read all my prayers.
Maybe answer some if He thinks they will benefit me.
Bless all my loved ones, my enemies and me.
God you are the rose that blooms over and over again in me.
Through all the seasons Jesus you are the fragrance that surrounds me.
Oh how it feels so good when God walks into the room and cleans up my mess.
Oh how blessed I am when Jesus stand up for me making my heart freezes in place.
The greatness love of all is God He has with one touch melted all my sins away.
Listen; hear the Holy Ghost speak the truth.
God loves you.
In Jesus name, Amen

103

Doors and rooms

We walk in and out many doors some are good some are bad.
Life will always try too closed us up in the wrong rooms.
God is that key that keeps us from getting locked up behind the wrong doors everyday of our lives.

My first door love took over the room.

My second door brought tear to my eyes pain would not release me.

My third door so many smiles, so much laugher, a shoulder to lean on and the comforting consoling hands that dry all tears.

My fourth door lost me somewhere in the room.

My fifth door found me in every corner, everyplace and behind the pictures.

My sixth door fear chases me around the room.

My seventh door understanding touched me and forgiveness carried me in its arms.

My eighth door, hate pushes me into the wall and anger pulled me around and threw me down.

My ninth door truth follows me in every part of that room.

My tenth door, unforgiving grew up all over the walls and lies surrounded the room in the dark.

My eleventh door joy jumped out took my hand and we danced across the room

My twelfth door was open wide and Jesus was setting there waiting for me.

My thirteenth door I saw my soul in God's arms as he walked away.

All these rooms have taught me a grate lesson.
We will see the good, but we will have to take the bad alone for the ride.
We can't hide from the world we must face are fears.
I found my way to Jesus.
Now if we knock down these walls we had built around ourselves.
Then I hope we would find the hallway that leads us straight to the arms of God our Father.
In Jesus name, Amen

104

You are the prayer in me

 You are the hope in my dreams.
I feel you holding my heart in you hand.
Oh how I need you Lord.
You have chased my soul into your arms.
Now I know which way to go in my life.
I need to keep your attention on me Lord.
Just love you with all of me.
I need you here always in my life.
You are the prayer in me.

I don't think I have never needed you so much.
My heart aces for you.
My soul calls on your name as it echo in my heart Lord.
I can feel my spirited Scream your name throughout my soul.
Hope with all my heart to here you answer me.
So please hear my cry and find away to be here by my side.
I will do anything you ask of me for only you can have my heart Lord.
You are the prayer in me.

God you walk around me with every step I take.
Your protection has caught my life in your web of love.
I believe you are the need in me everyday.
You have lifted my pain on the other side of the door locked away.
I give all glory to the Father, the Son and the Holy Ghost.
Amen to the Father, the Son and the Holy Ghost
Bless is those who love God with there hold heart forever, just like me.
You are the prayer in me.
In Jesus name, Amen

Prayer of my Heart 3-105

Lord I want to speak with you

Lord, I want to set down and speak with you.
Just talk for a while face to face.
While you hold my trimming hands tightly in your hand.
I don't want to be afraid when I speak my peace.
I believe my soul would finally come to rest.
For just one time in my life I get to set down with you God and have you to myself.
I want to have a real conversation with my Father.
I have a lot of question.
Lord I know you have all the answers.
I am trusting in you.
I need to understand.
I need to believe in me.
I need to know who to forgive all my enemies.
I must get this pain of my chest.
I must release this vengeful and judgmental heart to you Lord.
My ears are wide open.
To hear each and every word you say.
I must place all my sin in your hand.
This will lift these burdens off my heart.
Then I can see that smile you have place on me.
Hearing your voice rejoice in me is an amazing feeling.
I'm so pleased that my Lord set down with me.
Oh how I learn so much from thee my Father, my Lord and my God.
Thank you for speaking with me Lord God.
I Jesus name, Amen

106

Praise is the Key to open God's heart

Praise is the Key to open God's heart.
His joy is the stopper to keep the door open.
God has willed the faithful to walk through that door.

Praise is the Key to open God's heart.
His joy is the stopper to keep the door open.
God has blessed the poor to walk through that door.

Praise is the Key to open God's heart.
His joy is the stopper to keep the door open.
God has welcomed the righteous to walk through that door.

Praise is the Key to open God's heart.
His joy is the stopper to keep the door open.
God has called the peacemakers to walk through that door.

Praise is the Key to open God's heart.
His joy is the stopper to keep the door open.
God has asked the forgiving hearts to walk through that door.

Praise is the Key to open God's heart.
His joy is the stopper to keep the door open.
God has directed those that live by His word to walk through that door.

Praise is the Key to open God's heart.
His joy is the stopper to keep the door open.
God has opened His arms to the meek to walk through that door.

Praise is always been the key to God's heart.
Through His joy is only way to get there.
Just have faith that God will always answer that door.
Every time you have the courage to knock for Him.
God has opened His arms to will his favored ones to walk through that door.
In Jesus name, Amen

107

The healer of healers

God has healed every sore I have ever had.
The pain has never last.
God touch has healed every pain in me.
The medicine was given by the hand of Jesus Christ our Lord and Savior.
The healer of healers has been here.

Jesus your touch has come alone and healed all my pain.
There are no more tears and you dried my eyes.
The healer of healers has been here.
Lord you are here to comfort me through it all.
The healer of healers has been here.

You have placed your understanding inside of me.
You washed my sins away.
The healer of healers has been here.
My heart and soul is open wide to your sweet forgiveness.
There are so many times you have walked my way and healed me.
The healer of healers has been here.

You have saved me from myself.
You have thrown harm's way out of the playing field.
The healer of healers has been here.
Your strength has followed me with every step.
Your power has helped me up the mountain.
The healer of healers has been here.

My voice has cried out your name Lord.
I can see your glory walking up to me.
The healer of healers has been here.
Your joy has made me a bed to lie down in and sleep.
Your shield of protection has covered me up.
The healer of healers has been here.

My heart has kissed you on your cheek.
My soul had fallen asleep in your arms.
The healer of healers has been here.
In the end His healing medicine was place in me.
I am carried by the gentle hands of my Lord.
The healer of healers has been here.
In Jesus name, A-men,

108

I just want to do your will God

I hope and I pray that I have learned not to let go of God's hand.
I don't want to be lost.
I don't want to step off the path.
I don't want to walk down the wrong way.
I just want to do your will God.

I hope and I pray that I have listened how not to let go of God's hand.
I don't want to be sad.
I don't want to fall off the path.
I don't want to walk down the wrong street.
I just want to do your will God.

I hope and I pray that I remember not to let go of God's hand.
I don't want to be unhappy.
I don't want to slap off the path.
I don't want to walk down the wrong road.
I just want to do your will God.

I hope and I pray that I hold on tight not let go of God's hand.
I don't want to be crying.
I don't want to walk off the path.
I don't want to walk down the wrong highway.
I just want to do your will God.
In Jesus name, Amen

109

Give him all Praise

Stand up testify what God has done for you.
Give Him all praise His strength has shown us the way.
God will always be here too pick us up, dust us off and God will follow us the rest of our lives.

Tell us how He gave you the power to move the rock out your way.
Give Him all praise His strength has shown us the way.
God will always be here too pick us up, dust us off and God will follow us the rest of our lives.

Show us how many doors He has open for you.
Give him all praise His strength has shown us the way.
God will always be here too pick us up, dust us off and God will follow us the rest of our lives.

Tell how He gave you the power to knock down those walls.
Give him all praise His strength has shown us the way.
God will always be here too pick us up, dust us off and God will follow us the rest of our lives.

Show us the strength He gave you to climb that mountain.
Give him all praise His strength has shown us the way.
God will always be here too pick us up, dust us off and God will follow us the rest of our lives.

Tell me how He moved the curves, the bumps and smooth out the road for you.
Give him all praise His strength has shown us the way.
God will always be here too pick us up, dust us off and God will follow us the rest of our lives.

Show us how He covered the big pot wholes in your path.
Give him all praise His strength has shown us the way
God will always be here too pick us up, dust us off and God will follow us the rest of our lives.
In Jesus name, Amen

110

Good has walked in the door

Good has walked in the door with a smile on His face and He kisses me on my cheek.
Erasing away all my sins and He said this is your new beginning.
Remember all those old mistakes.
That made you fall the first time.
That got you lost on that long winding road.
Now you have learned the wrongs you have done.
So as you travel this path with your head hell high, ear on plugged and eyes open wide to see where you are going.
For nothing or no one, not even yourself, can pull the wool over you eyes this time.
Good has walked into my life.

Good has walked in the door with a smile on His face and He kisses me on my cheek.
Wiping away all my sins and He said this is your new day.
Remember all those old lies you told.
That made you slap the first time.
Where I found you lost on that winding road.
Now you have learned the wrong you have done.
So as you move down this path with your head hell high, ear on plugged and eyes open wide just to see where life is taking you.
For nothing or no one, not even you can put those blinders down over your eyes anymore.
Good has walked into my life.
In Jesus name, Amen

111

His love is deeper and for real

Some say I love you, with an empty heart.
But when God said I love you.
His love is deeper and for real.
It is with the deepest part of His heart.
God love His child.

Some have fake tears falling down from there eyes.
They say I love you.
But the tears of joy that fall form Gods eyes.
His love is deeper and for real.
Singing I love you from the deepest part of His heart.
God love His child.

With a smile filled with lies.
They said I love you.
But the smile that God has will make your heart jump for joy.
His love is deeper and for real.
I heard God speak I love you.
I felt my soul fall into the deepest part of his heart.
God love His child.

Too many dry kisses place on your lips.
With a dry voice you could barely say I love you.
But God brought me His sweet kiss.
His love is deeper and for real.
God hugs me with his deepest part of His heart.
God love His child.

Love is deep and God love is deeper than anyone's love.
You can feel His love softly touch inside your soul.
The gentleness of His voice echoes throughout your heart.
We do need to be love deeply.
The only one that can love us that deep is God.
It don't matter how you look, what size you are, your wealth or fame He loves every part of us anyway.
God will love you deeper than you have ever been love.
Just open your heart.
His love is deeper and for real
God love His child.
In Jesus name, Amen

112

Grown by Gods love

This family is like a tree grown by the love of God.
Each branch has hope stretching out to you,
and every leaf believe in the Lord are Savior Jesus.
Grown by Gods love

If we grow in God than our family tree become strong.
Nothing can destroy anything God has made.
You are a good friend that will never give upon me.
The love that He has shown stands by your side everyday and night.
You must learn to forgive your family.
They are the one that is going to hurt you the most.
Our family wake's up knowing that every moment of our lives is grown by His love.
Grown by Gods love

Faith grows little baby tree all around the family.
Nothing God has touched can be moved.
When it is your heart God has touched.
With God your family stays strong.
Grown by Gods love

Each day God strengthen us even more.
Too find all the answers through God.
Too keep this family together.
Walking hand and hand with the Lord God.
Grown by Gods love

God is holding my family in His arms every moment.
God is my tree that grows in my family.
His love feeds every part of my family,
and we grow even closer because of the word of God.
Grown by Gods love

Because God has lead us down this road together.
We may disagree but we understand one another.
If you don't have the heart to forgive then you have not found God.
We are a strong hearted family grown by the mercy of God.
Grown by Gods love
In Jesus name, Amen

113

Love

Love is so natural; it grows even more every day inside of your heart for that one love.
Nothing on this earth can come between the one you truly love.
It is a bond that is given by God. His love grows with your love.
That is why that bond is so strong. The power of God's love is a forever lasting love.

Love is a natural straight out of the heart. If you love someone and they do not love you back.
Let them go before anger takes over your mind.
Fighting, fussing, screaming will only bring you more pain.
Stop being a block in there way let them go.
Then turn to God His love can heal a broken heart.
Even in a damaged darken soul. His love can find those that are lost.
His love can bring a wondering soul back home.
If the love you have found is for real.
Then love them though God He can make your love stronger.
Sometimes the world will deal you a good hand with real love.
Sometimes you will be dealt a bad hand that brings you a fake heart.
But you should never be scared to give the love in your heart.
Even if it might get broken, but you just might come across the one that will love you back.
We must learn to pray for the right love. We don't want to miss out on that special ones love.
By holding back love from the one that really love you. Not except anyone that says I love you.
This new generation has abused these three words I love you.
So badly that it makes you question the one you love if they really telling you the truth.
If they love you just as much as you love them.
When you say these three precious words I love you.
One can only hope in every way you will always mean it.
Because only God knows what's in your heart and if the love you say you have is real.
To him love is the must powerful, cherished and kind blessing that God has ever given us.
To share with someone special in our lives is a true blessing.
Love is something no one can take from us as long as are hearts beat there will always be love in it.
As long as you keep you heart filled with the love God gave all of us the moment we was born.
It can bring us pain for as long as we hold that pain.
It can bring us joy that breathes as one in our lives forever.
We are the one that make are hearts harden, because of the pain someone left behind in us.
We must find away to forgive that one how broke your heart.
We must not let love die in us, but keep our hearts open for love.
Let love flow as far as it can into God and back into you.
Learn to love more things than you find to hate.
Stop crying over spilled milk, wipe it up and move on with your life.
Keep on believing and look for that special love.
In Jesus name, Amen

114

Stop

Stop trying to be God, because God did not put you in charge of nothing.
Stop saying God only looks like you.
Stop turn around grow up be a man stop blaming everyone for your problems.
Stop depending on everyone to make it to the top.
Stop being mean just to be mean.
Stop saying anything to inflict pain to someone feelings.
Stop making fun of those that eat a little more than you.
Stop punishing those that make one mistakes they are human.
Stop making your life more than what it is always tell the truth.
Stop jumping in and out of bed with to many friends.
Stop lying when you don't have to lie.
Stop acting like you are holy than thou.
Stop being a busy body sticking your noise in every ones business.
Stop spreading that nasty gossip around.
Stop taken those drugs that the doctor did not prescribed for you.
Stop drinking to much of the tainted water setting in your own drunken stew.
Stop playing with God He is no joke.
Stop judging the world before you get judged.
Stop acting like you better than everyone when you are as broke as the rest of us.
Stop beating on them that can't fight back.
Stop talking behind everyone's back face them.
Stop always frowning smile before your face get stuck like that.
Stop putting yourself in the wrong place at the wrong times.
Stop taking things that are not your.
Stop oh you evil one, using the church to hide behind the devil.
Stop giving up your body girl to everything that stands in your face.
Stop leaving you children out there on there alone.
Stop holding on to your unforgiving heart seek God.
Stop hating everyone because you have lost the one you love.
Stop quoting the bible when you what to make yourself look good.
Stop being a false witness to against your neighbors.
Stop punishing anyone more than you will punish yourself.
Stop acting like you are the only one that love's God.
Stop being Unholy and start being what God wants you to be.
In Jesus name, Amen

115

You need to call on God

Why must we walk around with anger pouring out our hearts?
You need to call on God.

Mad at everything and everyone.
You need to call on God.

Not smiling always frowning.
You need to call on God.

No laugher in your life is always sad.
You need to call on God.

Being unhappy with everyone you come in contact with.
You need to call on God.

You always greet everyone with a bad attitude.
You need to call on God.

Your jealousy has made you unbearable to be around.
You need to call on God.

Making up and spreading lies.
You need to call on God.

Always rolling your eyes as you mumbling as you pass by us child.
You need to call on God.

Acting like the world owes you something.
You need to call on God.

When you are ready to turn on the light, change your life.
You need to call on God.
In Jesus name, Amen

116

You are as one

Everywhere God goes.
The Son and the Holy Ghost they are right there by His side.
You are as one.

He may climb the mountains.
They will be with Him every step of the way.
You are as one.

He may walk down the street.
They follow closely behind Him.
You are as one.

He moves the rock.
They are there to help Him push it out the way.
You are as one.

He stands on the mountain top.
They are there by His side.
You are as one.

God set on His throne.
They will set down by His side
You are as one,

God is the Father, Jesus is the Son and there is the Holy Ghost.
Together they are as one.
In Jesus name, Amen

117

Remember, God is a jealous God

So you bow down your soul giving up your body for fortune and fame or for a little change.
So you bow down your soul for that drug that keeps you high from the troubles in your life.
So you bow down your soul to step on everyone for that power put's you in control.
Remember, God is a jealous God, but also God is a Forgiving God.

So you bow down your soul for lust that walk away leaving his family to struggle on there on.
So you bow down your soul to hold that gun that kisses your freedom goodbye young life.
So you bow down your soul for love that steals your old heart blind.
Remember, God is a jealous God, but also God is a Forgiving God.

So you bow down your soul to worship those false pictures, statues and walking idols.
So you bow down your soul to live in sin the lie is the truth and the truth is the lie.
So you bow down your soul to false profits, fortune-teller, palm-reader and psychic.
Remember, God is a jealous God, but also God is a Forgiving God.

So you bow down your soul to that shiny car, the big house on the corner, to all those worldly procession.
So you bow down your soul for that bottle that makes you happy.
So you bow down your soul to the dark side of the light and all that God has turned His back on.
Remember, God is a jealous God, but also God is a Forgiving God.

So you bow down your soul to be a false witness against your neighbor.
So you bow down you soul to a lie when you tell someone you love them and you don't.
So you bow down your soul when you turn you back on God the Father.
Remember, God is a jealous God, but also God is a Forgiving God.
In Jesus name, Amen

118

He set me free

For a long time I wonder through my life.
For a long time doors would not open for me.
For a long time I had got lost in the worldly things.
Then you walked up with a smile on your face.
He set me free.

For a long time I had took all the glory for my success.
For a long time I thought I was running my on life.
For a long time I thought I open these doors on my own.
Then I knocked on that door I have never stood before and there you were waiting for me.
He set me free.

For a long time I thought I had remove all the walls around me.
For a long time I thought I had been walking down this road alone.
For a long time I thought I removed the rocks that blocked my way.
Then I found you God, being the strength in me. To knock down all those walk that blocked my way.
He set me free.

For a long time I thought I made it through the hard time on my own.
For a long time I thought I was the one that put the food on my table.
For a long time I thought I was the strength that carrying me through each day.
Then I felt your power enter my soul teaching me how not to walk on my own.
He set me free.

For a long time I thought I was on the right path with my life.
For a long time I thought I did not need anyone to help me.
For a long time I thought God did not love me anymore.
Then I felt your love rise up out of my heart and hug my soul.
He set me free.

For a long time I thought God did not hear my prayers.
I found my answers waiting for me each and every morning.
When God makes it a point to wake me up and bless me with another day.
He set me free, from myself.
I Jesus name, Amen

119

He has blessed the fountain that runs in me

God I can feel you slowly move through my veins.
Into my heart you softly move through every part of my heart.
Into my soul you gently touch every part of my soul.
You woke up feeling that I never though I would ever feel.
He has blessed the fountain that runs in me.

The light in me got brighter than it ever been.
God has clean my soul with His love.
God has washed my heart with His peace.
God has thrown out all my sins out of me into the darkness were they need to be.
He has blessed the fountain that runs in me.

He drowns any wrong that lives in me.
He has pulled out the lies that have planted themselves in my soul.
He has swept the house He has built in me out with His mercy.
God has set free His forgiveness roaming around in me.
He has blessed the fountain that runs in me.

God has played a song of His love that echoes in me,
God has washed me down every part of me with His hope,
My faith in me follows Him all over my soul,
I believe now that God has always carried me in my life,
Now all I breathe is God, because forever He lives in me,
He has blessed the fountain that runs in me.
In Jesus name, Amen

120

Cause God knows my Heart

I believe He is already going by what is in my heart.
He seems to answer before I asked.
So if my heart was not in the right place I don't think God would have answered my prayers.
There are times I wonder if He here my prayers and the answer was stirring me in the face.
So if my heart was in the wrong place I don't think God would have answered my prayers.
You can see me walk down this road it seem like I am alone, but God know that He is there walking with me.
Cause God knows my heart.

So if my heart was not in the right place I don't think God would have answered my prayers.
You may think you have all the answers, but for me God is all the answers for the questions I had in me.
Each time I think of something I need God has already done it for me.
So if my heart was not in the right place I don't think God would have answered my prayers.
It may seem to you that I am making it on my own, but God is there holding my hand.
There are days that He has to carry me, Thank you God.
So if my heart was not in the right place I don't think God would have answered my prayers.
Cause God knows my heart.
In Jesus name, Amen

121

God knows what He was doing when He had gave us His only joy our Lord Jesus Christ.

I love you God.
I am missing something in my life.
I don't know what it is. Sometimes I feel unhappy, alone or sad.
But now that you have walked into my life I have found my joy.
Jesus still live among us and no matter were you are He is always there.
God knows what He was doing when He gave us His only joy our Lord Jesus Christ.

I Love you God.
I am very sorry for hurting you my Lord, I love you Jesus and you will always have my heart.
Life without you I'm just an empty shell wondering around until I die.
There is no one or anything as beautiful as you.
I know I let you down, but I beg of you to show mercy upon my soul.
Jesus let your forgiveness melt into my heart and soul.
The truth is that I need you to make my life better than I have.
God knows what He was doing when He gave us His only joy our Lord Jesus Christ.

I Love you God
Help my family, friends, my enemies and me to get back on the right path.
We have walked a longtime without your guidance in our lives Lord.
We can't go back and we can't go forward with out you leading us all the way.
There will always be a need for you my Lord Jesus in our life always and forever.
For He is the Holy church that worship in us every moment,
God knows what He was doing when He gave us His only joy our Lord Jesus Christ.

I Love you God
God please be with me and have mercy for my family, friends, my enemies everyday of our lives.
God you are all the hope we have and we need you all the time in our lives.
Keep your eye on us for there is no times we want need you.
There is not a moment we want need you to carry us and direct our lives in the right direction.
We will always need you to come find us if we lose our way home. God and Jesus thank you for hearing my prayer,
with the love from my heart proudly bow down to your heart God.
God knows what He was doing when He gave us His only joy our Lord Jesus Christ.
I Love you God
In Jesus name, Amen,

122

From my heart too your heart Lord

From my heart too your heart Lord,
I will breath in you.
I will hear your words.
I will love you.
From my heart too your heart God,

From my heart too your heart Lord,
I will hold you.
I will rejoice in your name.
I will believe in you.
From my heart too your heart God,

From my heart too your heart Lord,
I will bless your name.
I will praise your name.
I will forgive all.
From my heart too your heart God,

From my heart too your heart Lord,
I will glorify you.
I will hallelujah your name.
I will call on you for everything.
From my heart too your heart God,

From my heart too your heart Lord,
I will always pray.
I will thank you.
I will always be ready to do you will.
From my heart too your heart God,

From my heart too your heart Lord,
I will give you my soul.
I have given you my heart.
I will give you my life.
From my heart too your heart God,
In Jesus name, Amen

123

Love, Love you

Love runs deep in me for you Father.
God you built this love that grows forever in me everyday.
All I think about is you, because your love makes me so happy.
Each smile is full of love for you.
I have prayed for a lot of thing but your love is the best prayer I have ever received.
The spirit in me love you like no another love Lord.
The love I have for you is so deep in my soul.
Only God himself can find it.
My heart trembles at the sound of your name.
Love, love you,

I love you more the stars in the universe,
More than the sun has risen.
Deeper than the sea,
 More than all the water in the biggest ocean,
I love you more than the tallest mountain.
I love you; farther than the wind can blow.
Farther than a river can flow.
I love you more than I can breathe.
God more than my life,
I pray that my love melts everyplace in you Lord,
All the time,
Every moment of the day,
You are the one that keeps this smile on my face,
Love, love you

For my life,
You are the one that take care of me,
For all the many times you showed up for me,
Just being here before I asked,
Not just for all the love you have placed in my heart and not just for what you have given me in
my life.
I just love you God for being a good Father to me,
All the time, every minute of my life
Love, love you.
In Jesus name, Amen

124

Pain

To all those that hold on to pain, It time to throw it away, all that hurting must go out the window.

Are you still walk in pain, it is time to take off those hurtful shoes and throw then painful things out the door.

That pain got you crawling, it is time to get up dust off all that pain and walk again.

That pain has stolen your smile, you have painted a frown upon your face and it is time to wash the hurt and the pain down the grain.

That pain has ran away with your laughter, it time the make a joke out of all that hurt and bring back your smile,

That pain has kept your eyes swollen, tears dropping down you cheek, it is time the dry that pain up for good.

Has all that pain hardens your heart to God. God has all the answers to that pain and it is time to hand over all that pain to a healer our Lord God.
In Jesus name, Amen.

125

When the hand of God cleanses your sins

He started slowly forgiven me at my feet washing gently all the sins that has cling to my skin.
Removing all the sins that had crawled up under my skin trying to hide from God,
He went all the way to the top of my head.
Than God washed every strain of my hair one by one He washed my sins away.
When the hand of God cleanses your sins, you are free.

He moved himself inside of my heart pouring His forgiveness down into my blood, that running through my whole body.
You could hear the sins scream as God used the Holy Ghost to wash out my veins.
Then God cleans my spirit with His hands slowly removed all the sins that I had collected over years.
In just one moment God washed my sins away.
When the hand of God cleanses your sins, you are free.

He saves the best for last, the soul to wash with forgiveness with the Holy Ghost, all those hidden sins.
His hands slowly move all around picking up the sins that have stored themselves in my soul,
God found all those that had made there beds and they though they were home.
Until, God swept all those sins out the door.
My soul cried with joy, hallelujah God has Cleanse my sins and set me free,
When the hand of God cleanses your sins, you are free.

God has washed away all the bad and replaced it with His good, now the light of our Savior burns in me forever.
In Jesus name, Amen

126

Death broke my heart God

When you give birth to a child, you want to hold them forever.
There first step is so special. We will wait forever to here there first word.
Mama is hoping it is mama, Daddy is hoping it is dada.
Every moment spent with them is a gift.
We find ourselves not even willing to give them up to God.
Love still think life goes by our schedule, but when God come calling we must let go.
With water in your eyes, tear drops falling as you cry.
Slowly all the peace begins to fall.
Life shatters like glass. My heart hurt so bad Lord.
Death broke my heart God.

You believe in the one you love that they will be here with you forever.
When they are gone your life stops in place and they took your heart with them.
Everyone depend on you to make them feel better, but you can't please everyone when you are trying to deal with your own pain.
When pain grows inside of you, you are like a zombie running around.
Draining of life now you feeling so sick seem like you are dying too.
Because the one you love has passed on, leaving you behind to face life on your own.
Love still think life goes by our schedule, but when God come calling we must let go.
With water in your eyes, tear drops falling as you cry.
Slowly all peace begin to fall.
Life shatters like glass. My heart hurt so bad Lord.
Death broke my heart God.

I know you are the one with the love that never ends.
Lord you want take, your love back from us, even when we get lost.
Because your love helps us too fines our way back to you,
Sometimes we get tried of waiting on God, but God don't get tried of waiting for us.
It is call real love. When our hearts is put to the test, will we fail or will we show Him real love.
I looked away my sister was gone. I turned around my brother did not say goodbye.
Oh, in a blink of an eye God came through and took my life with him.
Will we be ready when God come calling.
Love still think life goes by our schedule, but when God come calling we must let go,
With water in your eyes, tear drops falling as you cry.
Slowly all peace begin to fall,
Life shatters like glass. My heart hurt so bad Lord.
Death broke my heart God.
In Jesus name, Amen

126

Picture the one you love, and watch the face of God smile back at you,

The color of your hair how long, how short and how it is moving when you walk.
Oh how beautiful the many ways you wear your hair.
The many ways you wrapped it up and the many ways you lay it down.
Picture the one you love, and watch the face of God smile back at you.

Moving down to you forehead, every mark and every scar that has touched your life shows.
Wrinkle telling us your life, dark spots, dark circles around your eyes, beautiful shin and every line that run under your eye.
Picture the one you love, and watch the face of God smile back at you.

Around your ears every curve, around to the back and back to the front.
Down to you ear lop, can you hear me when I say I love you.
Picture the one you love, and watch the face of God smile back at you.

Straight to your eyes, how many time you shaved your eye brow.
How long your eyelashes have grown and how many have fall into your eyes.
Your eyeglasses, changing your eyes with different colors of contact liens.
You can see as far as the sun raise.
You wink you eyes with a smile.
Picture the one you love, and watch the face of God smile back at you.

Running down to your noise, very long, a cute tiny one, and so big.
Runny noise, red from the cold, sneeze away you misery.
Picture the one you love, and watch the face of God smile back at you.

Move on to your lips, so big, so small.
Lips painted with many beautiful colors and some are plain as a blank screen.
A quit voice, a deep voice and always soft spoken.
A frown bent down, so sad, with a smile that brightens up a room.
Picture the one you love, and watch the face of God smile back at you.

Down to your chin, down to you neck, back around to you cheeks.
Rosy cheeks, very strong, very soft and with a moll on the right.
Few bumps, your pimple have dried up.
Now your face is young, smooth and clear.
But some day you will become old, your life will walk across will your face and your wrinkles
will show.
Picture the one you love, and watch the face of God smile back at you.

Now all your loved ones faces has come together.
How beautiful, how lovely, how sweet your smile,
Kiss upon their cheeks.
Picture the one you love and watch the face of God smile back at you.
In Jesus name, Amen

128

You breathe, they breathe, when God bless you with love keep your heart open wide

You breathe, they breathe, and no one can tear you apart.
Love touches the must gentle part of your heart.
All your mine can think about is them.
There is always a smile on your face.
That keeps your home warm with joy.
You barely can breathe when they are not around, even when they are just in the next room.
Your heart shakes, because you can still here there voice speaking to you even when they are not there.

You pray that God keep them out of harm's way.
Protect them from themselves and bring them home safely.
Were ever they maybe or were ever they may go keep walking with them my Lord Jesus.
A kiss upon your cheek, I whisper good night my love.
Just before we go to sleep I say a little pray that God be there to keep us safe every minute of the night with us as we sleep.
Once you awake the first thing you want is just to see the face God gave you to love.
As they lay there you watch them sleep.
You whisper thank you Jesus.
As there eyes slowly open there smile takes your breath.
Before you climb out of bed you say a prayer that God never leave your loved one or your side.

Let your angel protect them coming and going on every side in Jesus Amen.
They smile, they laugh and they giggle as they get dressed.
Tears come to their eyes as the say goodbye.
They dried them with their smile.
Sent through there day a way with a huge and a kiss upon their lips.
The day was lonely and with by fast slow.
There arms ache, longing to hold there love.
Greeted with open arms and with a big huge, a long lasting kiss.
With God nothing can come between or tares apart.
God hand has a strong hold on their love.
No pain can deceive, always drowning in hope.
God is the key to a wonderful lasting love and blessed life.
You should thank God for making your day.
Love only comes like this one in a life time.
You are truly lucky to know love.
You breathe, they breathe, when God bless you with love keep your heart open wide.
In Jesus name, Amen

129

But I know, I'm always in the need of God

It's good to walk in the light.
Nothing can go wrong.
Everything on this day was right.
I am happy, thank you God.
Joy feels the air with its glory.
My smile walks everywhere.
God you greet everyone with a big huge.
It doesn't matter how your life is going good or bad, day by day.
But I know I'm always in the need of God.

It is bad to wonder around in the dark.
God sometimes I find myself in trouble waters.
The waves seem to drown me in my own mistakes.
To carry me out to sea I am loss screams no one hears me calling.
Dealing with the stress, that drains my life.
Getting loss in my self, tried of digging my self out of my own problems.
But there is always a friend ready to carry me and if I get lost they are always there to fine me.
It doesn't matter how your life is going good or bad, day by day.
But I know I'm always in the need of God.

It's good to walk in the light.
Blessing runs all around me.
My head is healed up high.
I don't stumble over my own two feet.
I have not slipped.
The path is my friend, guiding me with His hand.
Finally love has opened the doors to my heart.
Love has been given wings now it flies through my soul.
Feeling like every part of me, has been touch by love.
It doesn't matter how your life is going good or bad, day by day.
But I know I'm always in the need of God.

It's bad to wonder around in the dark.
My heart has been thrown back and forth, kicked around.
Love has endeared to much pain don't want to show its face again.
My heart has closed up.
Life has so many trips and falls every time I turn around I am picking myself up again.
But there is a friend always standing next to me to be there to pick me up and dust off my sins one more day.
It doesn't matter how your life is going good or bad, day by day.
But I know I'm always in the need of God,
In Jesus name, Amen

130

God is the best part of my day

Thank you God for giving me the courage too change my ways.

I pray that God keeps His smile on me and always place His eyes forever upon me.

The Beginning is with God the Father, Jesus Christ our Savior and the Holy Ghost.
Love stand above all.
Hope wraps around my life.
Peace drains from my soul.
Joy takes over my hold body.
Forgiveness climbs all around inside me.
Understanding runs around inside my soul.
Kindness eats around my heart.
Blessed surround me forever.
Thanksgiving falls all over me.
Glory is the light that shines in me.
Good is only God and should only be handed out by God.
The Ending is with God the Father, Jesus Christ our Savior and the Holy Ghost.
God is the best part of my day.

I can love you by myself.
Then you may choose to love someone else.
But if I love you through God than it will last forever.
Selfish heart knows no love, just as un-forgiveness knows no forgiveness.
Do not live an empty lift.
Love all that God has put before you even when it hurt sometimes.
God is the best part of my day.

Watch God because he will be sending Jesus soon.
Don't hold you head, looking down.
Don't cover up your eyes at anytime.
Don't blink too much.
Open you eyes wide and look to the sky.
You may think it is the wind.
When it maybe Jesus passing you by.
God is the best part of my day.
In Jesus name, Amen

131

Love brings no pain

They can't bear to hurt you.
True love breathes the same air and lives the same life.
True love is a true blessing to have.
Love never wants to leave your side.
Don't want to see one tear fall from you eyes. Would rather die then too see you cry.
Travel across the world, will walk many miles to find you.
Love brings no pain.

Love is not lift at home or set aside when you decide to cheat.
If you truly love someone and they do not love you back than let them go with out harm.
Today I love you is so easy to say without meaning.
A closed heart cannot love or know how to love.
Remember you have the right to be happy.
Don't let know one take you smile, don't believe in there broken promises and don't let them get away with too many I'm sorry.
Now they can look you strength in the eye and lie to your heart.
Open up your ears hear the truth in their voice and lesson to your broken heart let them go.
Love brings no pain.

You can feel the realness in true love.
When that special touch come alone and touches your heart.
Something you have never felt before.
It has an everlasting holds on your heart.
When you find true love everything in your life is new.
When love, loves you back it feels so, so good.
Wrap like a ribbon around your heart.
Then you have found love and love has found you.
Everyone can see the joy that shows in your face and your eye gives your heart secrets away that you are in love.
It will move you into the arms of a wonderful love.
Love brings no pain.
In Jesus name, Amen

132

I will die for you

God has given us His only begotten son and Jesus' love has given us His life.
That our sins be forgiven forever.
Some many of us live by these earthly things and willing to seal our souls for it all.
Forgot about God, forgot about Jesus how He sacrifices His life.
Jesus did not have to sell anything He was just willing to give His life for us.
Know that God will give us his only joy and knowing Jesus is willing to die for me, I will die for you.

My Father, My Lord, My Jesus,
I will die for you.
I'll lay down my life.
Anyplace, anytime, anywhere,
I am the first one to go out to battle your enemies.
With my sword heal high.
I will strike them down with my life.
I will die for you.

All of your enemies, I will destroy them at you will.
I will stand on the front line.
Hold them back with all my might.
I will be that solder.
Give you my life.
I will die for you.

I am the shield.
That is here to protect you with my life.
I will let no harm come to you.
I will fight for your life and give you mind.
My Father, My Lord, My Jesus,
I will die for you.
In Jesus name, Amen

133

God

It is hard to wait on or to believe in God, but have faith. The reward is eternal life that is the glory of God.
Remember and never forget that you have a debit to pay.
Life is a gift from God, live it well, pray once a day and let your word be your bond. God is here always.
All sinners go to church and some are called saints. Many set in the front roll and shout Amen.
Maybe this Sunday they did not give because maybe they did not have it to give this time.
So you punish them when they are in need. God watches.
They will give a lot and the poor will give there last. Oh how the poor are truly bless with Thou Holy smile God's Joy.

Once they married for love passion smother there hearts.
Now they marry for lust a strong desire to have at any cost.
Hold on to God's hand and stop losing God in the crowd.
Look me in the eye and still you lie. So how now do I know were your heart is and how will I know if you are telling the truth?
Pray on it to God,

What I want is love beyond love. What I need is to be above my needs.
I want a best friend to be as one with me a good husband, for him a good wife.
God has blessed those that live by his vows.
We have walked that road, stumble down that path and climb that mountain, and God was always there by our side.
Everything that has gone wrong, keep your head up. Keep believe that God will make away.
I would not have been able to bare the pain without God walking me through it all, thank you.
I will not live by hate. I will not live in anger.
I will not live with revenge in my heart, but I will let God be my avenger.
I take your hand, you take my hand, you grab her hand, I will hold His hand and we will pray together with God.

Know more crying over spilled milk. Take all the punches.
Takes on all the kicks, but when you trap and fall, you don't give up.
Believe God is always holding your hand to pull you back up on your feet.
What makes us pure, being a virgin or not living in sin, a virgin can steal, lie and kill.
Because it is said we all are born in sin.
Be baptized in Gods eye by the blessing of his Holy waters.
To live not in sin, right cleanse your soul and God only knows how pure hearted we are,

What is ugly, what is pretty, so the out appearance catches our eyes?

So you get stuck in that dream world all over a pretty face.

You take that abuse an unhappy heart.

Ugly appear you frown upon that free happy heart God touches and bless all that we say is ugly.

Does it matter to God if you are ugly with a beautiful heart or beautiful with an ugly heart?

A smile that is looking down or a smile that is in everyone's face.

A quite voice shy, nerves and dare not to speak loud or a sweet voice that cries too gets all attention on them.

The question is who will be able to stand before God.

The ugly face with the beautiful heart or the beautiful face with the ugly heart.

Remember God don't like ugly. God judge you by your faith, your forgiveness and what is in your heart.

Walk with a kind heart with everyone.

In Jesus name, Amen

134

This is what I hope for you

This is what I hope for you. That Jesus walks with you everyplace.
That the Holy Ghost holds your hand at every turn that Jesus follows you everywhere.
That the grace of the Father takes every step with you, that God watch closely over you.
That Jesus take care you even when thing are going good. That all your bills are pay and food is always on your table.
That Jesus always find away to hold you in the palm of His hand. This is what I hope for you.

This is what I hope for you. That Jesus is with you through all the stormy days.
When you get lost He's there to light your way. That you see, hear the world though God's eyes and ears.
That Jesus doesn't leave you when you don't understand, that He gives you the understanding of all things.
That Jesus teaches you how to forgive with you hold heart. This is what I hope for you.

This is what I hope for you. That Jesus stand by your side when you travel down that road.
That you never be alone, He helps you find your own path.
To show you how to climb the mountain all the way to the top and always be there waiting for you.
To lie down next to you when you are sick or as you sleep.
To be the breath that a wakes you too a brand new day. That the sun always keeps you warm from the cold.
That God give you the warm rain that has the power to wash all your sins away.
I wish that you never have another bad day in your life. This is what I hope for you.

This is what I hope for you. To remove all your troubling times that may come your way.
To stand up too protect you from harm's way. To guide you through life by His will.
That you never be in need or want for anything in your life. That pain never comes into your life.
That Jesus dries your tears before they fall from your eyes.
That you don't know what is to cry over a broken heart. That God is always there to comfort you when your loved ones pass.
This is what I hope for you.

This is what I hope for you. That everything you touch God blesses it for you.
That God teach you what hope is all about with a prayer to guide you through life.
That you are always welcome into Gods open arms, that Jesus keeps you on His mind all the time.
That you know that truth can carry you alone way and set you free. That Jesus will teach you how not to let a lies touch you tong. That Jesus stops all bad thoughts from entering your heart that, He keeps them from come out of your mouth. I hope Jesus hold back your tong from speaking wrong against anyone including your enemies. That God give you the strength to keep the worldly things from braking you down. That Jesus will be your protection from all your enemies. This is what I hope for you.

This is what I hope for you. That you with all your heart always find away too embrace God.
That you never give up your smile or the laughter that moves in your soul.
Let no sorrow take away the happiness that you carry in your heart. That Jesus smile upon you always.
That Jesus teaches you to learn to take the bad with the good.
That you learn not too make a wrong out of a right. That you keep your hands clean from all the temptations that comes in your life.
Never ever give upon yourself. That you stay strong don't let this world take away your dreams and anything you want to be.
This is what I hope for you.

This is what I hope for you. That Jesus wraps His arms around you forever.
That Jesus teaches you to live by His word and walk in His way, That God hugs you everyday.
That God show you what love really feel like with His heart being a part of your heart?
That God give you a good life, in the name of Jesus Christ our Lord and Savior.
This is what I hope for you.
In Jesus name Amen.

135

You are always on my mind

I think about you all the time.
You are the prayer that repeats it self in my mind everyday.
Because I love you Lord, every minute of my life.
I breathe through you, with everything I do.
You are the smile that wakes my heart; you are the laughter that brings my soul so much joy.
You are the happiness that always echoes across my mind.
You are always on my mind, Lord.

I think about you all the time.
You are the prayer that repeats it self in my mind everyday.
Because I love you Lord, every moment of my life.
I breathe in you, with every part of me.
You are the life that wakes my heart; you are the voice that brings my soul so much joy.
You are the only name that always echoes in my mind.
You are always on my mind, Lord.

I think about you all the time.
You are the prayer that repeats it self in my mind everyday.
Because I love you Lord, ever hour of my life.
I breathe all of you, with everything in me.
You are the touch that wakes my heart; you are the kindness that brings my soul so much joy.
You are the peace that always echoes in my mind.
You are always on my mind, Lord.

I think about you all the time.
You are the prayer that repeats it self in my mind everyday.
Because I love you Lord, every second of my life.
I breathe just for you, with everyday that you give me.
You are the presence that wakes my heart; you are the hope that brings my soul so much joy.
You are the melody that always echoes in my mind.
You are always on my mind, Lord.

I think about you all the time.
You are the prayer that repeats it self in my mind everyday.
Because I love you Lord, everyday of my life.
I breathe your love, with every vine of my heart.
You are the will that wakes my heart; you are the smile that brings my soul so much joy.
You are the love that always echoes in my mind.
You are always on my mind, Lord.
Love you God.
In Jesus name, Amen

136

All you have ever been to me is a perfect friend

All you have ever been to me is a perfect friend.
Lord, oh what kindness you have shown to me in your heart.
It carries me with all the joy my heart can hold or hopes for Lord.

Lord, your there for me when I need someone to talk too.
Always listening or hearing my prayers with an open mind every word I say and not judging me
in anyway.
With carrying arms wrapped around to comfort me.
All you have ever been to me is a perfect friend.
Lord, oh what peace you have given to me in your heart.
It carries me with all the love my heart can hold or hope for Lord.

Lord, when I'm down I can call on you anytime.
You never once turn me away day or night.
Without question you would come right over and rescue me.
All you have ever been to me is a perfect friend.
Lord, oh what gentleness you have delivered to my heart.
It carries me with all the blessing my heart can hold or hope for Lord.

Lord, your shoulder is always there for me to lean on.
To hear your caring voice of hope with all the right answers.
I know I can depend on you every moment of my life.
Cause you went out your way to show me how to smile and how to keep happiness living in side me.
All you have ever been to me is a perfect friend.
In Jesus name, Amen

137

We'll be missing you

Lord your child has passed away, on this very day.
Another child has heard your voice calling.
That child caught an early flight.
Carried away by there our wings into the light, God has called His child and we'll be missing you.

You broke many hearts when it was said you were gone.
Did we hear it right, they must be wrong?
As the news help you wave goodbye, as tear fall from many eyes.
We remember watching you dance, it seem like you moved across the air.
I seem like you feet never touch the ground.
When you sing, your voice took over the room and many went wild when they spoke your name.
Many cried, yelled your name over and over, many tear poured out their love for you.
God has called His child and we'll be missing you.

This is the last song that will be written by you.
This is the last time many will hear you sing a song.
God has called His child and we'll be missing you.

This is the last note that will be written by your hand.
This is the last rhythm that will be played by you.
God has called His child and we'll be missing you.

This is the last steps and turns that will put together by you.
This is the last dance that many will see danced by you.
God has called His child and we'll be missing you.

This is the last time many will really here your voice for real.
This is the last time many will really see your face for real.
God has called His child and we'll be missing you.

Your music shell always play on, as you dance across the T.V, screen.
Many will cry, as they watch with there hearts.
God has called His child and we'll be missing you.
I Jesus name, Amen

138

Tear Drops Fall, Tear Drops Cries (1)

Tear Drops prayers for her child and hope in every way they live their life right
and do good thing with their life. You only get one life child please live it right.
We only can hope that child learn to hide behind God every time the devil walk there way.

Lord another Tear Drop is going to need your shoulder tonight.
Cause an unforgiving heart, a mad soul has come through and has taken another child life.
There is a sad song sing in the air tonight you can feel the many Tear Drops Fall.
That child want be coming home. Tear Drop Cried, to God, she still feel that last kiss those cold lips.
That soft feeling a sweet child lifts upon her cheek. Just before that child step out that door.
She remembers hearing that child say.
I love you Tear Drop that memory caused a chill to fall all over the room. Across her heart a deep
sorrow grows.
She holds on to the jacket that child last wore and that it still carries that child warmth.
Can still see those big brown eyes in her mind and hear that child voice hunting her dreams.
Can't sleep cause when she close her eyes all she sees is that beautiful face smiling back at her.
That child's laughter echoes forever in the walls of Tear Drop's heart.
Her face is so steel she doesn't blink with a waterfall running down her face.
She hopes one more time if she could wrap her arms around that child. Just too see her child one
more time running
through this old house. Eyes lock on the door hoping that child walks on in.
But her heart melts even more knowing that child want be walking through that door anymore.
That child has died, that child has given up on its life, that child has thrown away their freedom
and that child has runaway from home.
Lord says a prayer for that child. Walk with them every single day of their life. God you are the hope that
child will see tomorrow. Tear Drops Fall, Tear Drops Cries, God say a prayer for all the
Tear Drops tonight that prays for that child,

Only God know the pain that run through Tear Drop's vain. The new stuck her soul down on her knees;
she trembles as she said Oh God. Her voice let out a quite scream and she cried out her child's
name. As tears run down her face, like a river running wild. Her voice got louder; you can feel
her tears drowning the pain in her heart. She lost her voice with all that crying. Tear Drop
whispered, a live that barely has begun is
gone. Why someone would take away my beautiful life. The moment she hear the news, she
couldn't remember if her
heart has ever aced this much in her life Lord. Tear Drop said, she remembers that day like it was
yesterday it is still locked in her memory. She whispered no one has ever broken my heart until
now.
My Lord God there no greater pain when a Tear Drop loses her child.

That child had die, that child has given up on its life, that child has thrown away their freedom, and that child has runaway from home.

Lord, say a prayer for that child. Walk with them every single day of their life. God you are the hope that child will see

tomorrow. Tear Drops Fall, Tear Drops Cries, God say a prayer for all the Tear Drops tonight that prays for that child.

Tear Drop Fall, Tear Drop Cries, like a hard rain, a storm feel with grief began to takes over her life. The

lighting keeps going off in her mind. For many days pass before the cloud stop crying a clear day appears in

her eyes and the hand of the sun finally dry up her face now she can see. Her life stop walking around in a

daze, but her heart remember the love she once knew that child will never be forgotten. An echo in her

heart repeats that child name over and over miss you child. There is not a day that passes that she doesn't see your picture

run across her mind. Child you are the broken peace that fell out of Tear Drop's heart and her heart will never be able to

replace that peace of love lost forever.

Tear Drop hopes and prays for this young heart too think before they do wrong. Love too do right child. Love your life child.

Love your freedom child. Love too come home child. Love to not break Tear Drops heart.

Lord, say a prayer for that child. Walk with them every single day of their life. God you are the hope that child will see tomorrow.

Tear Drops Fall, Tear Drops Cries, God say a prayer for all the Tear Drops tonight that prays for that child.

In Jesus name, Amen

139
Number-1

Tear Drops Fall, Tear Drops Cries (2)

God hear Tear Drop's prayer; keep her child from play with the devil tonight.

Don't let the evil set his eyes on that child, God, Don't let evil harden another child's heart.

Lord, hide them from the devil's touch, don't let another child soul leave theirs eyes cold.
Don't let the devil whisper in that child's ear that it is ok to give up on their life.

Child lesson too your Tear Drop. Be a good child and hold on to the kindness in your heart.
Don't get lost in the streets. Don't go down the wrong road. Don't play with your life you only have one.
Stay young as long as you can don't grow old before your time. Don't give up on your young life.
Don't give away your freedom. Stop running away from your problems face them head on and don't let evil get in side your head.
Know who you are. Never lessen too what the devil has to say. Learn to walk away from the confession.
Gangs don't bring you no protection and remember you already have a family. A lot of love is waiting for you in the
arms of your Tear Drop. Believe in your shelve and trust that your Tear Drop will always be there for you. Tear Drop love's her child.

God protect that child from themselves, their enemies and keep them far from harm. Hold them Lord closer
to your heart. Say a prayer for that child. Walk with them every single day of their life.
God, hear Tear Drop's prayer. Make time for that young child. Guide those young feet, protect their young
hearts and souls. Teach their minds to live there dream and no matter how hard it gets never give upon yourself.
Maybe if God build your church in their hearts letting it over flow into their soul.
Tear Drop hopes and prays for this young heart too think before they do wrong. Love too do right child. Love your life child.
Love your freedom child. Love too come home child. Love to not break Tear Drops heart.
Lord, say a prayer for that child. Walk with them every single day of their life.
God you are the hope that child will see tomorrow.
Tear Drops Fall, Tear Drops Cries, God say a prayer for all the Tear Drops tonight that prays for that child.
In Jesus name, Amen

140
Number-2

You are the one that holds my smile

Each morning I wake up to another day.
I don't know what this day has in store for me.
Blindly we all walk through life.
Knowing not what waits for us around each corner.
I just know Lord; you are the one that holds my smile.

As I leave this old comfortable house.
I don't know if I am coming home again.
Are if this old house will still be here waiting for me.
Unexpected thing happen especially when we are not ready for the storm to come through.
I just know Lord; you are the one that holds my smile.

I'm happy because I know that in this world there is someone that love me with there hold heart.
I know they are the ones that give me strength.
They always believe in me more than I believe in myself.
Life can take you in too many circles; some doors open and some remain closed forever.
I just know Lord; you are the one that holds my smile.

No matter what go on in my life I always make time to say a prayer.
Asking God, too walk me through the problem that may rain down on me.
No one can ask for a better friend like the Father.
Good and bad spirits will come in and out of your life some will take, some will give.
Pray for right, pray to send wrong on home, in your life try your best to do it right.
I just know Lord; you are the one that holds my smile.

I know to give my troubles to God before I try to fix them myself.
He is the answer and all I have to do is lesson when he speaks to my heart.
I know my life set in His hands and if I die today.
Those that love me will remember me in there hearts as a good person.
I just know Lord; you are the one that holds my smile.
In Jesus name, Amen

141

God hear my Heart

There is a song that sings deep in my heart.
That make's the soul shout out hallelujah.
All praise to the Father.
God hear my heart.

There is a sweet sound a melody that moves deep in my heart.
That make's the soul cry out its blessing.
I give all peace to the Father.
God hear my heart.

There is a soft whisper that roams deep in my heart.
That make's the soul show off its Holy Spirit.
All glory to the Father.
God hear my heart.

The only pain I want to fell is the love that aces for you in my heart.
That makes the soul roll out it love.
I give all my life to the Father.
God hear my Heart.

There is a divine voice that calls out deep in my heart.
That make's the soul speak its joy.
All thanks to the Father.
God hear my Heart.
I Jesus name, Amen

142

Jesus said, Anger can't say in the presence of God

Lord understanding doesn't live in this world anymore.
Lord move this inflamed anger from our Souls.
Out of weakness an angry fire burns in our Hearts.
Jesus teaches us understanding with a kind heart.
I don't want to be lost and left behind.
I don't want to carry unforgiving heart or give up the presence of God that surrounds my life.
Jesus said, Anger can't say in the presence of God.

Lord Forgiveness has lifted our heart behind.
Lord helps us there is a strong emotion that is screaming in our Souls.
We are filled with anger kicking hard in our Hearts.
Jesus teaches us forgiveness with a kind heart.
I don't want to carry unforgiving heart or give up the presence of God that surrounds my life.
Jesus said, Anger can't say in the presence of God.

Lord Thankfulness has dries up inside of our soul.
Lord, please be by our side a wrath of anger is raging in our Souls.
We go into a furious feeding the madness in our Hearts.
Jesus teaches us thankfulness with a kind heart.
I don't want to carry unforgiving heart or give up the presence of God that surrounds my life.
Jesus said, Anger can't say in the presence of God,

Lord the children have a lot of anger a rage that has spilled blood all over there Souls.
There young lives have built a strong emotion in their flaming Hearts.
Lord wash theirs soul with every tear that falls from your eyes.
Put out the flame with the love in your tears.
Dry up the anger from us all Lord.
I don't want to carry unforgiving heart or give up the presence of God that surrounds my life.
Jesus said, Anger can't say in the presence of God.

Lord, Father the world is very angry full of madness.
We must pray in name of the Father to keep the anger away.
When anger come knocking learn to closed the door in it face.
Give all to God; let the Lord touch our Souls.
Because anger can't stand in a room filled with Goodness.
It can't sleep in the same Heart with God.
I don't want to carry unforgiving heart or give up the presence of God that surrounds my life.
Jesus said, Anger can't say in the presence of God.
In Jesus name, Amen

143

Because we haven't learned to just wait on God

We pray asking God to help us with our dreams.
Maybe finances, careers or bring love in our life.
But do we wait for our answers from God.
Are do we move on with our dreams in the wrong direction.
We think everything we have we got it on our own.
Some think it luck when good thing come there way.
Everything you wanted falls in place.
Patting yourself on the back think you have done this on your owe.
But when the walls start too fall.
The doors don't open anymore.
All your calls go unanswered.
Bad news keeps coming for you in every direction.
Braking down your dreams you have built for your life.
All you friends say I'm sorry to hear you lost it all.
When they were just all waiting too see you fall.
Wondering what happen when all go wrong blaming everyone else, but yourself.
You look back at your life and cry why.
Because we haven't learned how to just wait on God.

We find ourselves wanting more at every turn.
Not happy with what we have lost our thankfulness in our greed.
We were gambling with our lives one more time trying too changing the out come.
Just to lose once again.
Playing with our lives will soon bring us down to realty.
When life teaches you a lesson about yourself learn for it.
How to learn and grow from all the way you have failed yourself.
I say why we fall just to get up and try again.
But only this time with the help of God at our side to get it right the first time.
Because we haven't learned how to just wait on God.

Remember give God a chance to answer your prayers.
Don't forget about God let Him be the one to lead your life.
God has a shoulder for you to lean on.
God has open arms to comfort you at anytime.
God is the friend that will always be there to pat you on the back when everything is going good,
He is there to pick you up when you fall a good friend to help you get back on your feet again.
God is the voices that say get up and let us try this again together.
We would be stronger if we just learn to wait on God.
Because we haven't learned how to just wait on God.
In Jesus name, Amen

144

God must have a reason to take you with him,

I have never seen a smile that moved around the world.
Oh how many chase this smile to just catch a glimpse of your face.
Tears fall from their eyes just at the sight of you.
Don't you dare cry, say goodbye, say so long and now you're gone.
There will be a new star in the sky tonight.
God must have a reason to take you with Him.

The song you were singing has come to it ends.
The music stops moving your feet.
All the noise of the crowd has stopped calling your name and has walked away.
I have never seen eyes as sad as yours, tears that cry hidden inside.
Only God knows the pain that is lock behind the mind of a beautiful song.
Don't you dare cry, say goodbye, say so long and now you're gone.
There will be a new star in the sky tonight.
God must have a reason to take you with Him.

God has given us a beautiful song; we just didn't play it enough.
But you tried to give us more life then you had to give.
Through all that pain you tried to sing that beautiful song once again.
But the pain in you knocked on God door.
Don't you dare cry, say goodbye, say so long and now you're gone.
There will be a new star in the sky tonight.
God must have a reason to take you with Him.

I never have seen a life that made the world cry.
All your fans that waited a long time in line just to here your voice again.
I never saw you so happy when they all scream your name.
Don't you dare cry, say goodbye, say so long and now you're gone.
There will be a new star in the sky tonight.
God must have a reason to take you with Him.

When all those waving hands have stopped clapping I see your sadness fall across your face.
The hold room become still, you can here a pen drop.
The curtains come down and the lights go out; your smile went to a frown.
I have never seen eyes as sad as yours, tears that cry hidden inside.
Only God knows the pain that is lock behind the mind of a beautiful song.
Don't you dare cry, say goodbye, say so long and now you're gone.
There will be a new star in the sky tonight.
God must have a reason to take you with Him.
In Jesus name, Amen

145

Knowing Jesus you saved my life with your life every day

Jesus you died upon a cross that we may be forgiven of ours sins.
At that moment it was the first time you saved my life with your life.

Today is a good day.
Everything is going my way.
Good new keep coming around me.
A big smile painted on my face.
I am so happy.
Nothing can go wrong for me.
Everything right is falling into place for me.
All that I know is here to help me in anyway I need.
But the only joy I have in my life today.
Knowing Jesus you saved my life with your life every day.

Each day I open my eyes.
I awake with you lying by my side.
The joy in me can only hear a soft spoken voice whispering I love you.
Knowing Jesus you saved my life with your life every day.

Each night I closed my eyes.
You lay down next to me.
The joy in me can only see your face smiling back at me.
Knowing Jesus you saved my life with your life every day.

Today is a very bad day.
I woke up on the wrong side of the bed.
Today must be a Monday.
No good new have came by to see me today.
My smile has turned into a frown, because my tears have broken my heart.
When things are going right there is a crowd around me.
When thing go wrong no one calls.
All that you know find thing to do to keep away from you.
But the only joy I have in my life today.
Knowing Jesus you saved my life with your life every day.
In Jesus name, Amen

146

Cause you are my hero every moment God

I have always counted on you.
Lord all through my life.
You are always there to save me from myself.
Never letting harm come my way.
You have kept my enemies at bay.
I was once lost in the dark.
You came along, took my hand, and led me into the light.
Cause you are my hero every moment God.

There has been time I felt along.
But God you shook my soul to let me know your right here.
When I felt ill too sick to get out of bed, you carried me and laid me down in your healing arms.
The heart arc that pours in my soul, your kindness dried up the pain in my heart.
By morning I was healed by you will.
Now I'm strong all the weakness in my soul is gone.
Cause you are my hero every moment God.

I have lost everything that I had.
All that I own is gone now lift with nothing.
Maybe I cared too much about earthly things.
A lesson to learn that earthly things come and go has no soul.
You taught me that you are what we need.
You are the blanket that gives me warmth from the storm.
I trust in your words.
My hunger is feed by your love.
You are the shelter that walks with me through life.
Cause you are my hero every moment God.

I want to be found in your heart, drowning in your love.
I took one step to you and you took two steps to me.
We met face to face at the flock of the road.
You said follow me now down the right road.
It is good to know that I am moving in the right direction, because of you God.
I just want to always be apart of your life God.
You will always have a straight line to my soul.
I will never let you leave my heart not for one second.
I Love you with all of me, forever in my life you shell be.
Cause you are my hero every moment God.
In Jesus name, Amen

147

The Love of God has brought me home

The love of God has followed me throughout my life.
If God stop loving me it would break my heart forever.
Who will I call on, who would I turn to, how lost would I be without you God.
I choose to stumble with no one but God down this road.
 I learn that I don't walk this life without God or on my own.
Hand and hand, step by step, side by side down this road with God.
I freely give my life to God's will.
Just guide me in your way I will do as you say Lord.
I have felt the warmth in your arms, Lord.
As I feel your hug tightens up around me. I feel you bring me closer to your heart.
I can here the beat of your heart calling me Lord.
Your spirit has drained all my love into you.
All through my mind I only hear your name God.
I have melted into your soul.
My life has humbled itself to your will.
Living in your peace has covered my life with your joy.
I'm happy to see that I walk your path with you Lord.
The un-selfness in me forgives all those who troubled me
That my spirit may release the power of those that hate me to understand forgiveness.
I got to be able to forgive for God to be able to see my heart.
I don't want to live my life without the forgiveness of God.
Watching over me every step, every turn and every move in my life you are there by my side.
I don't have to scream your name when I need you Lord.
I softly whisper your name Lord then you are here.
It is good to know that I am not lost.
As long as God is here in my life I want live my life alone.
I believe in God, I don't want to be the one that die and wake up to late.
I want to know God now and die with him owning my heart and soul.
Then die not believing in Him just hear God say I don't know me.
God you are the light that pave's my way through life.
Now that I am lost in you God I never want to be found.
The love of God has brought me home.
In Jesus name, Amen

148

I believe Father you just saved my life again

God you have always been the brave one inside of me.
You are that push that helps me to not give up on myself.
Oh Lord your strength is what carries my spirit every step of my life.
For some reason we get lost when we lose the need for God, but God don't lose us.
Because when the devil tries to whisper in my ear, God closed him out of my life every time.
I believe Father you just saved my life again from myself.

God you have always been the force of power a voice inside of me.
You are the door that opens every time I knock.
I seek; I fine you in my soul. I ask than you were given to my heart.
Oh Lord your forgiveness shakes my soul. When I'm right or when I'm wrong you are there for me.
Something come over us we don't want God around, but God never leaves our side.
When the devil come knocking God's the one that answer the door for me.
I believe Father you just saved my life again from my enemies.

God you have always been the will that drives me to succeed living inside of me.
You are the hand that guides my life down the path secured by your righteousness.
Oh Lord you are the shelter that protected my life every day.
There are times we try to push God out of our lives, but God's there waiting to catch us before we fall.
When the devil blocks my path God you are the hand that moves the danger out of my way for me.
I believe Father you just saved my life again out harm's way.
In Jesus name, Amen

149

Can I walk with you God, Forever?

If I reach my hand out too you God, will you take my hand with out hesitation?
Can I walk with you God, forever?
Just to see where you will lead my soul.
I need to fine my path in you.
I will follow you God everywhere you go.
Keeping my eyes wide open never losing sight of you God.
If I blink I just might get lost.
Can I walk with you God forever?

If I call on your name Lord, will you answer me with a voice of concern?
Can I talk with you God, forever?
I just want to know how to live my life right.
To see through his eyes is to be able to speak the truth.
Let Him teach me with His will, always with an open heart.
To learn not to question everything that happens in my life.
Let it play out in Jesus name.
I will never close my ears to the sound of your voice Lord.
For I may fine that I have lost my way.
Can I walk with you God forever?

If I come knocking at your door God, will you open the door with haste with out making me wait?
Can I knock on your door God, forever?
Just to see how many doors you have open for me.
I ask you God to unlock the door that has all the answers.
Never give up on God he is the key to life.
Each door that is closed before me is open at God's will.
I want that key that take's me where I needed to be.
That only open's the right doors.
I don't want to step into the wrong life and lose my way.
For I may fine myself closed in forever.
Can I walk with you God forever?
In Jesus name, Amen

150

Father, Forgive Me

What do you do when you lose God on the way to Church?
You stop walking down the right road long ago.
Found yourself traveling down that trail of confusions.
Let your sins eating away at your soul too many years.
Do you fall down on your knees and pray.
At that moment you felt God pull away.
Did you scream Lord don't leave me.
The sun maybe shining outside, but rain from your eyes cries for God.
Here my voice calling your name Lord.
Father, forgive me.

What do you do when you lose God on the way to work?
I put all my time into this job.
I say, are you going to make it without God.
But every day that I raze up I am tried Lord.
I found out the hard way I can't live with out God.
I found myself traveling down this trail so lost in my soul with my eyes closed.
Do you raise your hands to shy were ever you are standing.
Beg God to hear the pain in your heart.
Lord, help me to climb my way out of the dark.
Let your light be my guide to you Lord.
I call out your name I'm here just see me Lord.
Just look my way my Lord.
Father Forgive Me.

What do you do when you lose God on the way Home?
You just set there watching the wall pull your family apart.
Fight your way through a crowd that you say you love with all your heart.
You found yourself traveling down this trail of despair.
Hopelessness is living in your soul for too many years.
Do you bring your family together bow your heads and pray,
God help us find our way back into your grace,
Please Lord has mercy for a wondering soul,
Make this family strong with your will Lord.
To walk the right path, to drink from your fountain that will cleanses our souls,
To find the right road that leads us home to you God,
Father, forgive me.
In Jesus name, Amen

151

Forgive

I saw the face that took the love of my life away.
It seems like my heart stop beating.
My tears ran like rain down my face.
My hearts just want to pray that God take you away.
Like the love you took from me.
God said, child find away to unhardened your heart.
Forgive, because an unforgiving heart want walk through the gates of heaven.
Forgive, release yourself take back the power they hold over you.

I have seen the face that took my child's life.
It is said you didn't even know my loved one name.
Just a drive by to prove that you are down for your newly found family.
Did you think this child must have a family that just maybe love them and would miss them if they died?
I cried, I scream at your face, my heart just want you to die.
Like the child you took from me.
God said, child find a reason to warm up your heart from the cold.
Forgive, because an unforgiving heart want be able to speak to God.
Forgive, free yourself take back the power they hold over you.

I seen those faces, stealing, kill and rob you blind.
You have broken too many rules.
Shell I lock you away and throw away key.
You took something you can give back to me.
My tears have dried up but the memory still live with me.
Pray that you never see the light of day.
God said, child find away to open your eyes with the key in your heart.
Forgive, because an unforgiving heart want be able to see God.
Forgive, release yourself take back the power they hold over you.

I saw that face that used me, broke my heart and try to take my dignity.
It hurt so bad a river ran in me and down my cheeks.
In my mind I tore up the memory that pictures of their face.
I prayed to find away to throw away all the love in my heart that I had for you.
God help me to clean up the tears that my broken heart left behind.
My heart can't help but hope that one day they feel the same pain.
God said, child find away to keep from letting anger erase the love in your heart.
Forgive, because an unforgiving heart can't be forgiven by God.
Forgive, free yourself take back the power they hold over you.

God taught us to forgive with my hold heart.
Forgive, because forgiveness has God sitting right here in our heart.
I took back the power they once had over me and now forgiveness lives in me.
In Jesus name, Amen

152

God, Jesus and I

God, Jesus and I we walk together in my life.
I can feel the peace Jesus has placed in me.
Trials and Tribulations can't follow me anymore.
Cause God has taken over my life.
There's not a day that goes by I don't think of you God.
Tears may fall from my eyes.
But I'm just letting the happiness pour out from inside of me.
You are the smile that appears on my face from no were.

God, Jesus and I we walk together in my life.
I can feel the Joy Jesus has placed in me.
Sorrow can't follow me anymore.
Cause God has taken over my life.
My heart is always asking about you Lord.
My soul seems to be lonely, because it's always miss you God.
Time may fly by, but you are always here by my side.
You're the light that never needs changing.
You are the flame that burns forever in my Soul

God, Jesus and I we walk together in my life.
I can feel the understanding Jesus has placed in me.
Suffering can't follow me anymore
Cause God has taken over my life.
Through your eyes I see your love growing in me.
You have sealed my spirit away in a safe place only you can go God.
Your soul slowly pushes life into my heart for keeps.
If you ask I will lay my life down to thee.
I believe you are everything I need in my life.

God, Jesus and I we walk together in my life.
I can feel the Holy Spirit Jesus has placed in me.
Unforgiving can't follow me anymore.
Cause God has taken over my life.
My life needs you to be apart of me Lord.
The secret is that my soul and my spirit have already runaway with your heart God.
Whatever you want I will freely give you every part of me.
I have already forgiven myself for even being one moment without you in my life Lord.
In Jesus name, Amen

153

Jesus you are the peace of mind

I set my heart, my life, my soul and my mind in your hands Lord Jesus.
I trust you to be here always by my side throughout my life.
Jesus you are the peace of mind in me all the time.

Warm affection,
A good friend,
Every precious moment,
Standing here by my side,
Holding me up too face life with your strength.
Jesus you are the peace of mind in my heart.

Devoted to God,
A good friend,
Every cherished minute,
Walk with me Lord, step by step with you by my side every day.
Holding me up to face life with your understanding,
Jesus you are the peace of mind in my life,

Deep divine love,
A good friend,
Every tender second,
Counting on you God, too always be here by my side.
Holding me up too face life with your forgiveness.
Jesus you are the peace of mind in my soul.

Filled with joy,
A good friend,
Every given day,
Blessed with you God, forever will be here by my side.
Holding me up too face life with your will.
Jesus you are the peace of mind in me all the time.
In Jesus name, Amen

154

With God in my Heart

With you God guiding my heart I will live by your will forever.

I carry the same forgiveness.
That God carry in His heart.
There no other Father.
I rather walk with you in my life.
With God in my heart, blessed truly am I.

I feel the same love.
That God feels in His heart.
There is no one but the Father.
I rather walk with you in my life.
With God in my heart, loved truly am I.

I desire the same peace.
That God holds in His heart.
There is only one Father.
I rather walk with you in my life.
With God in my heart, in Peace truly am I.

I will forever keep the joy.
That God has in His heart.
There will never be, but you Father.
I rather forever walk with you in my life.
With God in my heart, filled with joy truly am I.
In Jesus name, Amen,

155

Lord I pray for all our Heroes

Lord I pray for our firefighters, our police and our brave solders.

Lord I pray that they always see their enemies before their enemies see's them.

Lord I pray that they see all the danger before them before danger fall's upon them.

Lord I pray that the power of your strength gives them the courage to crush the ugly face of evil.

Lord I pray that your hand is always there to pull them out of harm's way.

Lord I pray that all our Americans Heroes at home and far away.

Lord I pray that you always be there to protect them and keep them safe.

Lord I pray that your light always be their to guide then through all the dark places,
 down those roads of uncertainty and God always be the prayer that finds their way back home.

Lord I pray Thee to bring them home to there waiting family.
In Jesus name Amen

156

You are my smile

God I try each day to bring my life a little closer to you.
Because sometime I still get lost in these worldly things.
But there are day that everything just falls in place for me.
My soul laughs because it's happy.
I Trust in you Lord, to always make away for me to see a blessed day.
Take my love Lord.
Do as you wish with it.
I give you my heart.
I don't know why you have blessed me so many times.
But I know God at the end of the day you are my smile.

God I pray each day to bring my life a little closer to you.
Because there are still times I find myself wondering down the wrong path.
But most of the times I find myself walking the path you prepared for me.
My joy is to see your light shine in me.
I Trust in you Lord, to be there.
Take my love Lord.
Do as you desire with it.
I give you my heart.
I don't know why you have been by my side so many times.
But I know God at the end of the day you are my smile.
In Jesus name, Amen,

157

Waiting for me

Most of my life I have been fed by your words.
I pray for your love.
I pray you save my soul.
Let your joy rise up into my spirit and just hold me there in your presence.
Let my life lay in your hands.
Let me sleep in your grace.
I want to feel your warmth move around in me.
As you walk every moment in my life.
I need you Lord to be there before I ask.
I know in my heart Lord you are more than a wish that has come true in me.
You are the love that brings tears to my eyes.
Your touch make's my heart cry.
My soul feels the laughter in you run into me.
Now I know what it is like to be happy.
Your love has filled the thirst in my heart.
My life has chosen to bow down at your feet.
Into your open arms my soul runs.
You are the promise that keeps it word.
I want get a broken heart by loving you Lord.
At the end of every road that I travel, I believe that you God will always be waiting for me.
In Jesus name, Amen

158

Father Love You

Father you are my fallen star.
Your love is what my heart wish for.
The warmth of your love has protected me from the storms.
My love forever lies down in your arms.
Only Jesus knows how much my heart love you.
Father Love you.

Father I count on you to lead my heart in your direction.
Lay down your path for my love can follow you every moment.
Thank you for planting your love in me.
Only Jesus can see how beautiful your love grows in my heart.
Father Love you.

I don't know who not to love you Father.
My heart is always open to you Lord.
The more love you are willing to give my heart God.
Only Jesus knows how my heart needs too be apart of your love.
I want to be overwhelmed with your love running through me every day of my life.
Father Love you.
In Jesus Name, Amen

159

I Felt God

There was a time my worries had consumed me.
I just want to wakeup with my heart filled with his joy.
Until my spirit reach out to God, I never felt His power until He touch me.
I shook uncontrollable and it seem like my soul lifted out of me.
Then I walked in the spirit world.
Hand and hand with my Lord God.
While peace poured over me.
I held God in my arms just for a moment.
Now I know how it feels.
To be touched by God.
In my heart, in my soul and in my spirit I felt God.

There was a time an illnesses had over come me.
My spirit could not breathe on its own.
Until my spirit reach out to God, I never felt His power until He touch me.
I shook uncontrollable and seem like my soul lifted out of me.
Then I walked in the spirit world.
I stood side by side with my Lord God.
While his mercy poured over me.
I lay in his arms just for a moment.
Now I know how it feels.
To be touched by God.
In my heart, in my soul and in my spirit I felt God.

There comes a time my soul need more.
Longing for a better relationship with God
My life thirst for his touch, the hunger in me can only be feed by God.
Until my spirit reach out to God, I never felt His power until He touch me.
I shook uncontrollable and seem like my soul lifted out of me.
Then all the songs of my heart poured out into His arms.
Every part of me began to praise His name.
While his joy poured over me.
I wrapped my life in His arms forever.
Now I know how it feels.
To be touched by God.
In my heart, in my soul and in my spirit I felt God.
I Jesus Name, Amen

160

Pray my sins away

We must live, eat and breathe God Father, The Son and The Holy Ghost.
The way the world is leading us into destruction with the way we live our lives.
Wrong is right and right is wrong.
We turn our backs on God without think about the consequence.
Lost in what's on the other side of the fence.
God I give you all and every sin in me.
Pray my sins away.

God we know you don't like ugly, we must clean up are lives before God close his eyes against us.
We can't hide from God or hide our sins.
We must stand up and ask for forgiveness.
Pray and hand over our sins to God.
He knows what to do with them all.
Cause he is the love that forgive His child.
Pray my sins away.

Learn to cry away your sins into God arms.
Give Him the pain that keeps the anger.
Let Him be the one to dry your sins away.
God forgive me for the wrong in my life.
Pray my sins away.
In Jesus name, Amen

Prayer of my Heart 4-161

I Found my Treasure

I found my treasure in Jesus heart.
I found my soul guided by Jesus will.
I found this song written in my heart.
By my Lord, Jesus Christ,

All I think about is Jesus,
All I care about is Jesus,
All I hope about is Jesus,
And all I need is God the Father to guide me in his way.

Blessed is the Lord,
Blessed is Jesus,
Blessed is the Lord,
Blessed is Jesus,

And I praise my God the Father,
And I praise my Lord, my Lord Jesus Christ,
And I praise my God the Father,
And I praise my Lord, my Lord Jesus Christ,

I found my joy in Jesus heart.
I found my life guided by Jesus will.
I found this melody written in my heart.
By my Lord, Jesus Christ,
In Jesus name, Amen

162

Carry me Home

Jesus, don't leave me standing here alone.
Sometimes we get lost.
Thinking we can walk on are own.
It so hard too find our way back in the dark my Lord.
Shine your light.
Take my hand.
Pick me up.
Carry me home.

Jesus, don't forget about me.
Hear my prayer don't turn way from me.
Somehow I let go of your hand.
I left your side walked off the path and went the wrong way.
Thinking I could stand on my own.
I'm truly lost Lord without you by my side.
Carry me home.

Lord please, don't pass me by.
Sometimes we slip, fall in ourselves and can't get up on our own.
No matter how hard we try, just fall back down again my Lord.
Shine your light.
Take my hand.
Pick me up.
Carry me home.

Thank you Lord.
You shined your light for me.
You took my hand and helped me back onto my path of life.
You came to me when I fell and you picked me up.
Please, God make it your business to always come and find me when I get lost.
Then carry me Home.
In Jesus name, Amen

163

Why I Love to Write about the Lord

Too keep the peace and love in my heart, mind and soul.
That I may love everything about this world as it is.
That I may, love everything about the people of this world as they are.
I pray that we all find away to always be kind,
 care about what we say and have a nice hello too all that we meet in our lives.

That our Lord Jesus Christ.
Bless those who desire peace in their lives and in their hearts.
Too see the world through his loving heart and his eyes of forgiveness.
In Lord Jesus Christ Blessed name Amen.

164

Oh Most High

Only you can see the pain in me.
Catch me before I fall.
Only you can dry my eyes with your joy.
Only you can give my broken heart some peace.
Oh Most High

I just want to drown in your love forever.
To hold you close to my heart.
Let my love follow you down the right road.
Let me drown my life in your heart.
Oh Most High

The Father, with love unconditionally, for someone like me, blessed art Thou.
Let my praise rain down on Thee.
Oh Most High

Only you can feel the loss in me.
Make my heart beat with your mercy.
Make my heart fall in love with you everyday.
Only you can bless me with your love.
Oh Most High

I just want to breathe you in and out through every moment of my life.
To hold you close to my soul.
Let me breathe in your love.
Let my spirit sleep quietly in the warmth of your arms.
Oh Most High

The Father that has forgiveness, for someone like me, glory to Thee
Let my prayers always touch your heart.
Let me breathe in the spirit that owns my soul forever.
Oh Most High
In Jesus name, Amen

165

Anywhere, Anyplace, Anytime

There are times we find ourselves lost in this worldly life.
Through the struggles and falls it seems like we are still crawling.
There are times we can't find the peace in ourselves.
So worried and filled with fear, our eyes carry heavy tears.
So we look in all the wrong places, for our answers.
God when you have always been there in a prayer.

So I pray Anywhere, Anyplace, Anytime for you my Lord.
There is no time to get lost in myself.
I need you, right then and there.
I'm not ashamed to call on your name Lord.
So I pray Anywhere, Anyplace, Anytime, for you my Lord.

There are times when we think we are carrying these burdens all alone.
But I tell you that the Lord is the strength that carries me.
He is a Good God.
There are times we just don't think we can make it.
Not strong enough.
But I tell you, the Lord is our hope and the answer.
He will walk with us all the way.
Anywhere, Anyplace, Anytime, I call on you my Lord.
In Jesus name, Amen

166

Yesterday, New Day, Tomorrow

I asked the Lord God in Jesus name.
To forgive me for any sins I have done yesterday.
When we live in yesterday years all those memories harden the heart.
The pain, the love lost, the forgiveness and the unforgiving letting hate eats at our souls.
Yes, it's time to let go.
Let the Lord take care of the past.
You must live each moment in Jesus name, Amen.

I thank the Lord God in Jesus name.
For the breath that wakes me up to a new day.
When we are given a new day we are blessed with His will.
For the Lord God has breathed His breath in us.
Too see one more given us another chance to be forgiven of our sins.
That we have time to forgive those that wronged us.
You must live each minute in Jesus name, Amen.

Because our Lord God.
Has not promise us another day, but to cherish the time we have each new day.
In Jesus name, Amen
I praise the Lord God in Jesus name.
For giving me hope.
Not promising me that I will see tomorrow, but loving me today with His whole heart.
You must live every second in Jesus name, Amen.

We live our days thinking about what we are going to do tomorrow.
We lose time spent caring for our loved ones.
Drowning our soul worrying about what is going on tomorrow.
This is a day that may not come.
We are surrounding our lives in the future.
Wakeup be thankful for each day the Lord God blesses us to see.
Let us not get lost in ourselves.
Pray that we don't lose sight of what is real.
The love of God is always real and the love of our loved ones that really love us.
You must live each day in Jesus name, Amen.

167

The love in your heart Lord God

Sometime we set in the dark.
We let the light burn out.
We get so lost in ourselves.
We only can be found by you God.
By the love in your heart Lord God,
When the rest of the world judges us with unforgiving hearts, only He can find away to show us mercy.

There are times we are bad and do wrong.
We let the things in our life bring us down.
Where we lose our strength to get up and try again.
We only can be helped by you God.
By the love in your heart Lord God,
When the rest of the world judges us with unforgiving hearts, only He can find away to show us forgiveness.

We some times walk with a troubled heart.
We can't find where we left our peace.
We live our lives without a care for anyone or ourselves.
Only you can put a broken heart back together God.
By the love in your heart Lord God,
When the rest of the world judges us with unforgiving hearts, only He can find away to touch our hearts with joy.

Love is spread by the kindness in His heart.
Our hearts was blessed to feel the joy of knowing what love is like when it comes from God.
How the sweetness of His love pours out of His heart.
I would put all that I am and all that I love in God's hands.
By the love in your heart Lord God,
When the rest of the world judges us with unforgiving hearts, only He can find away to make us feel safe in His arms.
This is the love that comes from God.
In Jesus name, Amen

168

As we walk with them

God is our Peace.
Jesus is our Joy.
As we walk with them.
We don't have to worry anymore.

God is our Hope.
Jesus is our Faith.
As we walk with them.
We don't have to worry about getting lost.

God is our Mercy.
Jesus is our Strength.
As we walk with them.
We don't have to worry anymore.

God is our Guide.
Jesus is our Direction.
As we walk with them.
We don't have to worry about getting lost.

God is our Grace.
Jesus is our Life.
As we walk with them.
We don't have to worry anymore.

God is our Love.
Jesus is our Light.
As we walk with them.
We don't have to worry about getting lost.

God is our Praise.
Jesus is our Glory.
As we walk with them.
We don't have to worry anymore.

God is our Blessing.
Jesus is our Savior.
As we walk with them,
We don't have to worry about getting lost.

God is our Always.

Jesus is our Forever.

As we walk with them.

They will always be by our side. I shall never walk a trail alone or walk a path on my own.

Down the road of life I will carry my Lord with me.

I shall not stumble, I shall not trip, and I shall not fall without the arms of God ready to catch me.

I have the Father and the Son here at my side to give me the answer in my life at anytime.

As we walk with them we don't have to worry anymore.

In Jesus name, Amen

169

In Jesus name, I love you Father

In Jesus name I love you Father.
With all my heart you are what make's me breathe.
Each morning when His touch awakes my life I'm always found in His arms.
I Hope you are always there to bless my day.
I want to live in your presence forever.

In Jesus name I love you Father.
With my entire mind you are all and everything I believe in.
Your truth is every step I take; I trust you want let me slip.
I Hope you are always there to bless my day.
I want to live in your presence forever.

In Jesus name I love you Father.
With all my soul you are what make me live.
Each moment of the hour I'll just praise your name.
I Hope you are always there to bless my day.
I want to live in your presence forever.

In Jesus name I love you Father.
With all my love your first, the middle and last in my heart.
My soul thank you every second of my life each time I awake in your arms.
I Hope you are always there to bless my day.
I want to live in your presence forever.

In Jesus name I love you Father.
With all my life you are what make me breathe.
Each morning you're the first face I see, He's the one with the gentle touch that awakes me in His arms.
I Hope you are always there to bless my day.
I want to live in your presence forever.
In Jesus name, Amen

170

Carry Me

From my heart to your heart Lord Jesus,
I ask you my Lord Jesus to hear my prayers.

From my heart to your heart Lord Jesus bless me with your hope.
Stand by my side.
Hold my hand.
Carry me; until I find the strength in me to walk on my own.

From my heart to your heart Lord Jesus bless me with your light.
Hold me close in your arms.
Guide my life down the right path.
Carry me; until I find the courage in me to walk on my own.

From my heart to your heart Lord Jesus bless me with your peace.
Dry all my tears from my eyes.
Comfort my Soul.
Carry me; until I find the strength in me to walk on my own.

From my heart to your heart Lord Jesus bless me with your joy.
Drown me with your Love.
Lay me in your warm Heart.
Carry me; until I find the courage in me to walk on my own.

From my heart to your heart Lord Jesus bless me with you.
Hold me every moment in your arms.
Smother my life with your love.
Carry me, until I am just holding your hand as I walk not alone in my life.
In Jesus name, Amen

171

In Jesus name, I thank you God,

For the breath that wakes me up every morning.
You open my eye for me to see another sun rise.
Through your mercy you have granted me a new day.
In Jesus name, I thank you God.

For walking with me, step by step through the happy times.
Guiding me God through all the storms, all my fears and always there to dry my tears.
In my life I am gripped in your hand, with your mercy standing by my side.
In Jesus name, I thank you God.

For watching my loved ones, my friends and over me every moment I breathe.
All that I care for, keeping us out of harm's way.
For not answering every prayer, wish or hope in my heart.
Only answer the one prayer that benefits me in my life.
God you are always seating by watching over me throughout the night as I sleep.
In Jesus name, I thank you God.

He that breathes in me, He is complete, perfect, and is whole.
He is our Father everything about Him is excellent, and there is nothing faultless about Him.
He is God the all Mighty one. Lord you are perfect in every way and in all directions.
In Jesus name, I thank you God for giving us you.
In Jesus name, Amen

172

In Jesus name

In Jesus name, God hear my prayers.
You don't have to answer them all.
God I love you with all my heart, my entire mind, all my soul and all my might.
God look at me don't walk away. God I love you.
Just answer the prayers that will help me in my life each day you breathe in me.
In Jesus name, Amen

In Jesus name, God hear my prayers.
Don't close your ears to my prayers.
God I believe in every part of you Lord.
Watch over my children and all that I love, Lord.
Take care of all our needs and make sure you are there with us every second of a day.
Guide us and keep us from harm's way. God I love you.
I give you all glory, blessed is your name.
All beauty to our Lord God I give Him all praise.
In Jesus name, Amen

In Jesus name, God hear my prayers.
You don't have to answer them all, just ones that will help me in my life.
God I love you. Jesus is always, all the time and forever in my life.
Be with us everywhere, because we need you every moment.
Shelter us with your strength too help us go on living in you.
Comfort our tears, release our pain, and let us lay in you arms.
Never ever let us go. God look at us. Don't turn away.
Just answer as many prayers with your heart.
Let it be your will each day we awake that you be the one to bless us,
Remember me, remember them and remember us in your prayers Lord.
I know we have sinned against your children, ourselves and sometimes you Lord.
Help us, forgive us and believe that our hearts have change for you Father.
Have mercy and love us with all of you Lord.
In Jesus name, Amen

173

I Sing a Song

I sing a song from deep in my heart that praises His name.
Only you Lord can hear that voice, singing deep in my heart.
That thanks you God the Father.
The Most High for being here in my life.

I sing a song from deep in my soul that glorifies His name,
Only you Lord can hear that voice, singing deep in my soul.
That thanks you God the Father.
The Most High for being here by my side.

I sing a song from deep in my heart that blesses His name.
Only you Lord can hear that voice, singing deep in my heart.
That thanks you God the Father.
The Most High for being here in my life.

I sing a song from deep in my soul that rejoices His name.
Only you Lord can hear that voice, singing deep in my soul,
That thanks you God the Father.
The Most High for being here by my side.

I sing a song from deep in my heart, that sing hallelujah too His name.
Only you Lord can hear that voice, singing deep in my heart.
That thanks you God the Father.
The Most High for being here in my life.

I sing a song from deep in my soul that exalts His name.
Only you Lord can hear that voice, singing deep in my soul.
That thanks you God the Father.
The Most High for being here by my side.

I sing a song from deep in my heart that magnifies His name.
Only you Lord can hear that voice, singing deep in my heart.
My soul thank you God the Father.
The Most High for being here in my life.
In Jesus name, Amen

174

Praise God

I was nothing without you Lord.
I would be lost without you in my life Lord.
We stumble, we slip and we fall off the path of life.
When I lift your side I was lost Lord.
You are the light that shines in me, Praise God.

Praise God in Jesus sweet name.
Praise God for giving us Jesus our Savior.
Praise God for His joy, His only begotten Son.

I was nothing without you Lord.
I would be lost without you in my life.
Was blind, was deaf and was lost on a lonely road.
When I lift your side I was lost Lord.
You are the light that brighten up my path that lead me back too you, Praise God.

I was nothing without you Lord.
I would be lost without you in my life.
We live in pain, we live in fear, and we live in darkness, within ourselves.
When I lift your side I was lost Lord.
There is no living light that's there to walk us home when we get lost.
He is the one that makes time to come and find me before the end of the day or before the sun goes down, Praise God.
I hope that He be the one that finds me when I get lost every time, Praise God.
In Jesus sweet name, Amen

175

But, I love the Lord

How can anyone not believe in you God?
With all the love you have for us in your heart.
He died upon a cross for us, beautiful Savior.
How can anyone not believe in you Jesus?
With all the love you have for us in your heart.
Lord, you give us your breath each new day.
There is no another love that clings to our hearts.
But, I love the Lord, with all of my heart.

How can anyone not depend on you God?
With all the mercy you have for us in your heart.
How can anyone not depend on you Jesus?
With all the mercy you have for us in your heart.
Lord, you guide us as we stumble into you arms each new day.
There is no another love that clings to our soul.
But, I love the Lord, with all of my heart.

How can anyone not trust in you God?
With all the forgiveness you have for us in your heart.
How can anyone not trust in you Jesus?
With all the forgiveness you have for us in your heart.
Lord, you catch us before we slip and fall each new day.
There is no another love that clings to our lives.
But, I love the Lord, with all of my heart.

I will never stop believing in my Lord.
He is my heart, He is my soul.
He is everything that I want to be growing forever in me.
He is the sacrifice that laid His heart upon the cross our beautiful Savior.
But I Love the Lord, with all of my heart.
In Jesus name, Amen

176

Everlasting to Everlasting is God

Everlasting to Everlasting is God.
You are my hope to make it through a day Father.
You're the smile that's on my face when I think of you Father.

Everlasting to Everlasting is God.
You sleep in my heart.
My soul is your pillow.
I shall seek your face Lord, forevermore God.
Don't slip; don't fall always there by my side to catch me God.
So lead me on forward by the will of your right hand God.
Into your loving arms, is where I want to be, is always forever with you God.

Everlasting to Everlasting is God.
You are my hope to make it in this life to be able to see tomorrow Father.
You are the need that is in my soul that wants you more in my life Father.

Everlasting to Everlasting is God.
You are my hope to make it through the night Father.
You are the comfort I trust that you will be there to watching over me, while I sleep next to you Father.
In Jesus name, Amen

177

Jesus I will follow you

You die up on the cross for the forgiveness of our sins.
How beautiful are Thou heart.
Too love us with your life my Lord Jesus Christ.
You are the morning that finds us a new day.
You are the light that shines in the night that shows the way home before we get lost.

Jesus I will follow you
down that road, down that path
anywhere, anyplace and anytime my Savior,
your comfort is like a shelter from a rain storm.
Your joy brightens the way to your open arms.

Jesus I will follow you
down that road, down that path,
anywhere, anyplace and anytime my Savior,
your tears cleanse a trouble soul.
Your voice woke the love that slept in this sorrowful heart.

Jesus I will follow you
down that road, down that path
anywhere, anyplace and anytime my Savior,
your love is like a river that never ends.
Your arms are like the warmth that falls from the sun.

Jesus I will follow you
down that road, down that path,
anywhere, anyplace and anytime my Savior,
your hold over my heart makes my love bow to your every need.
You are the life that awakes in me everyday.
In Jesus name, Amen

178

Nothing good but God

Counsel me in your word Father.

Counsel me in your commandments Father.

Counsel me in your mercy Father.
God I love you.
Nothing good, but God

Cleanse my soul in your kindness Father.

Cleanse my soul in your grace Father.

Cleanse my soul in your gentleness Father.
God I love you.
Nothing good, but God

I sought you with my hold heart.
Found you standing there by my side Father.

I sought you with all my might.
Found you watching over me Father.

I sought you with all my soul.
Found out you have always been here Father.
God I love you.
Nothing good, but God
In Jesus name, Amen

179

Blessed is the Savior, Jesus Christ

I am sorry when I brought pain to your heart.
When I made you sad tears filled form my eyes.
My heart calls out for you too forgive me for all my sins.
Lord you can see in me.
Take the selfishness in me away.
Blot the wrong out in me.
Teach me who to walk in the Father's way, Lord.
I truly love you, Jesus.

Blessed is the Savor, Jesus Christ, Hallelujah Thou name.
You are the only heart, who cares enough to die upon a cross for the forgiveness of our sins.

Blessed is the Savor, Jesus Christ, Hallelujah Thou name.
You are the only one, who has a Holy Father with so much mercy to give us His only joy.

Blessed is the Savor, Jesus Christ, Hallelujah Thou name.
You are the only one heart we can go through to be forgiven of our sins.

Blessed is the Savor, Jesus Christ, Hallelujah Thou name.
You are the only one who has the right ears for our Holy Father to hear our prayers.

Blessed is the Savor, Jesus Christ, Hallelujah Thou name.
You are the only heart who will give us the breath that will wake us up to another day.

Blessed is the Savor, Jesus Christ, Hallelujah Thou name.
You are the only one, who knows the right path for our lives.

Blessed is the Savor, Jesus Christ, Hallelujah Thou name.
You are the only heart, who knows the direction to bring us home to you.

Blessed is the Savor, Jesus Christ, Hallelujah Thou name.
You are the only heart that breathes life in us day after day.
In Jesus name, Amen

180

Sing a Song

Sing a song that feed your heart with the Glory of God the Father.
Sing a song that feed your soul with the Joy of God the Father.

I felt a sweet melody come out of my heart.
I am singing about your glory my God the Father.
How gentle you are in my life, Jesus Christ.
Your kindness runs through the vines in my heart.
A melody pours out your forgiveness Lord upon me.
There is no one who will comfort me with his grace.
You magnify the song in my soul with your touch.
You are the tremble that shakes me deep in my whole soul.
Making my soul echo all praise, to your name Father.

Lord Feeling your mercy cleanses my soul.
Your voice Lord meditates in my heart.
You are my heroes that grow the strength in me.
Day to day, night by night, you are my salvation.
There is an echo singing a song over and over through my soul blessing the Father.

Your song moves into my heart blessing our Lord Jesus Christ, Our Savor.
You voice come singing too me in my dreams singing don't forget who truly love you.
I want let anyone take your song God out of my heart.
Give all missed notes to God and sing your song to our Lord Jesus with an open heart.
Trust in the Father and Son they will always be there for you.
In Jesus name, Amen

181

Lord of Lords, God of God

When I am in my lowest state I call on you.
Lord the strength of your mercy fell upon me to stand up on my feet.
I don't want to worship someone that can't fill me.
Because in my soul your touch lives in me He is the Lord of Lords, God of Gods.

I don't want to worship someone that can't breathe.
Because in my heart your breath life in me He is the Lord of Lords, God of Gods.

I don't want to worship someone that can't see me.
Because in my soul your eyes see all my desires He is the Lord of Lords, God of Gods.

I don't want to worship someone that can't eat.
Because in my soul your words fed me until I was full He is the Lord of Lords, God of Gods.

I don't want to worship someone that can't speak to me.
Because in my soul your voice echoes around in me He is the Lord of Lords, God of Gods.

I don't want to worship someone that can't show me mercy.
Because in my soul your mercy gives me strength He is the Lord of Lords, God of Gods.

I don't want to worship someone that can't hear me.
Because in my soul I know your ears are open wide to hear my prayers He is the Lord of Lords, God of Gods.

I don't want to worship someone that can't move me.
Because in my soul your present move thought the vein in my heart He is the Lord of Lords, God of Gods.

I don't want to worship someone that can't forgive me.
Because in my soul your love is the only love that forgives my sins He is the Lord of Lords, God of Gods.

I don't want to worship someone that has no soul.
Because in my soul your life grows forever in me He is the Lord of Lords, God of Gods.

I don't want to worship someone without a heart.
Because in my soul your heart beats with my heart He is the Lord of Lords, God of Gods.
There is no way, No how, I will give you up.
You are my thanksgiving, my salvation, my every thing forever.
He is the Lord of Lords, God of Gods, all my love to you always.
In Jesus name, Amen

182

Praise God, Bless Jesus

Praise God with all my heart for He is my life.
Bless Jesus with all my soul for He is my Savior.

Praise God with all my heart for He is all my salvation.
Bless Jesus with all my soul for He is all my Joy.

Praise God with all my heart for He is my strength.
Bless Jesus with all my soul for He is all my glory.

Praise God with all my heart for He is all my praise.
Bless Jesus with all my soul for He is all my mercy.

Praise God with all my heart for He is all my happiness.
Bless Jesus with all my soul for He is all my gladness.

Praise God with all my heart for He is all my forgiveness.
Bless Jesus with all my soul for He is all my courage.

Praise God with all my heart for He is all my comfort for all my sorrow.
Bless Jesus with all my soul for He is all my laughter that dries my tear.

Praise God with all my heart for He erases away all my sins.
Bless Jesus with all my soul for He is all my protection,

Praise God with all my heart; bless Jesus with all my soul.
Praise God, Bless Jesus will all my love too Thee.
In Jesus name, Amen

183

God is good

Let us humble ourselves to God.
With all our hearts let us blow to His glory.
God is good.
Let us humble ourselves to God.
With all our souls let us blow to His salvation.
God is good.
Let us humble ourselves to God.
With all our might let us blow to His forgiveness.
God is good.
Let us humble ourselves to God.
With all our hearts let us blow to His perfection.
God is good.
Let us humble ourselves to God.
With all our souls let us blow to His power.
God is good.
Let us humble ourselves to God.
With all our might let us blow to His blessing.
God is good.
Let us humble ourselves to God.
With all our hearts let us blow to His excellent.
God is good.
Let us humble ourselves to God.
With all our souls let us blow to His thanksgiving.
God is good.
Let us humble ourselves to God.
With all our might let us blow to His mercy.
God is good.
Let us humble ourselves to God.
With all our hearts let us blow to His affection.
God is good.
Let us humble ourselves to God.
With all our souls let us blow to His worthiness.
God is good.
Let us humble ourselves to God.
With all our might let us blow to His righteousness.
God is good.
Let us humble ourselves to God.
With all our hearts, with all our souls and with all our might let us blow to His praise.
God is good.
In Jesus name, Amen

184

His love is my Joy

In my heart the most precious love is Jesus our Savior.
His love is my Joy.

In my heart the most understanding love is Jesus our Savior.
His love is my Joy.

In my heart the most forgiving love is Jesus our Savior.
His love is my Joy.

In my heart the gentlest love is Jesus our Savior.
His love is my Joy.

In my heart the most perfect love is Jesus our Savior.
His love is my Joy.

In my heart the most splendid love is Jesus our Savior.
His love is my Joy.

In my heart the most faithful love is Jesus our Savior.
His love is my Joy.

In my heart the most blessed love is Jesus our Savior.
His love is my Joy.

In my heart the true love is Jesus our Savior.
His love is my Joy.

In my heart the most purist love is Jesus our Savior.
His love is my Joy.

In my heart the most worthy love is Jesus our Savior.
His love is my Joy.

In my heart the most favored love is Jesus our Savior.
His love is my Joy.
In Jesus name, Amen

185

God is good

Every time His breath wakes us up.
Every time we see another morning.
God is good.

Anytime His mercy carries us through our sorrows.
Anytime we see the faces of our loved ones.
God is good.

All the times He has been there to catch us before we fall.
All the times He has kept us out of harm's way.
God is good.

Every time He opens our eyes to see another sunrise.
Every time we see a beautiful sunset.
God is good.

Anytime His love carries us safely home.
Anytime we see God in the faces of our loved ones.
God is good.

Always He is there to find us before we lose ourselves.
Always there too keep us going in the right direction.
God is good.
In Jesus name, Amen

186

But Jesus

Sometimes we find ourselves lost within ourselves.
There's no one to find our hiding place, but Jesus.

Sometimes we find ourselves in deep sorrow within ourselves.
There's no one to find comfort for our pain, but Jesus.

Sometimes we find ourselves all alone within ourselves.
There's no one who will help complete our lives, but Jesus.

Sometimes we find ourselves in harm's way.
There's no one to save us from ourselves, but Jesus.

Sometimes we find ourselves doubting our will to be strong within ourselves.
There's no one to give us enough strength, but Jesus.

Sometimes we find ourselves walking without hope within ourselves.
There's no one to bless each and every step we take down our path, but Jesus.

Sometimes we find ourselves seeking peace within ourselves.
There's no one to show us true love, but Jesus.

In Jesus name, Amen

187

I hope God

I hope God smile on me everyday.
That His presence strongly surround's me.
All the time, anywhere, everyplace my path may carry me.
That God be there to direct my mind forever.

I hope God keeps His eyes on me everyday.
That His presence strongly surround's me.
All the time, anywhere, everyplace my steps may lead me.
That God be there to guide my soul forever.

I hope God always walk with me everyday.
That His presence strongly surround's me.
All the time, anywhere, everyplace my life may bring me.
That God be there to direct my love forever.

I hope God keep His ears to my prayer everyday.
That His presence strongly surround's me.
All the time, anywhere, everyplace my day may take me.
That God be there to guide my life forever.
In Jesus name, Amen

188

I trust in you Father

I believe in you with all of me God the Father.
With all my might I trust in you God.
Love that overflow from you Lord into my heart.
Your forgiveness shelters my soul Lord.
God rescued me from all of my iniquity.
With all my life I trust in you Father.

I believe in you with all of me God the Father.
With all my might I trust in you God.
Love that meditates from you Lord melts into my heart.
Your gentleness shields my soul, Lord.
God rescued me from all of my iniquity.
With all my life I trust in you Father.

I believe in you with all of me God the Father.
With all my might I trust in you God.
Love that magnified from you Lord falls into my heart.
Your righteousness saved my soul, Lord.
God rescued me from all of my iniquity.
With all my life I trust in you Father.
In Jesus name, Amen

189

God I pray Thee to teach me how to do your will

Guide my life with your word.
Show me how to walk in your way.
Lead me down your path of righteousness.
Give me the strength to keep me from stumbling.
Without you God my soul will become lost.
God I pray Thee to teach me how to do your will.
In Jesus name Amen.

Guide my life with your commandments.
Show me how to live in your grace.
Lead me down your path of righteousness.
Give me the strength to keep me from stumbling.
Because without you God my soul will become mislead.
God I pray Thee to teach me how to do your will.
In Jesus name Amen.

Guide my life with your obedience.
Show me how to be more like Thee.
Lead me down your path of righteousness.
Give me the strength to keep me from stumbling.
God without you my soul will become astray.
God I pray Thee to teach me how to do your will.
In Jesus name Amen.

190

The Father, the Son and the Holy Ghost

Blessed are the Father, the Son and the Holy Ghost.
Come into our lives.
Teach us how to keep our lives in your direction.
Let your spirit move in us.

Glorified are the Father, the Son and the Holy Ghost.
Come into our lives.
Teach us how to keep our lives in your grace.
Let your spirit grow in us.

Excellent is the Father, the Son and the Holy Ghost.
Come into our lives.
Teach us how to keep our lives in your mercy.
Let your spirit be in us.

Peace is the Father, the Son and the Holy Ghost.
Come into our lives.
Teach us how to keep our lives in your light.
Let your spirit shine in us.

Love is the Father, the Son and the Holy Ghost.
Come into our lives.
Teach us how to keep our lives in your Joy.
Let your spirit be the strength in us.

Praise is the Father, the Son and the Holy Ghost.
Come into our lives.
Teach us how to keep our lives in your guidance.
Let your spirit be the force that lives in us.

Truth is the Father, the Son and the Holy Ghost.
Come into our lives.
Teach us how to keep our lives in your understanding.
Let your spirit be a comfort in us.

Thanksgiving is the Father the Son and the Holy Ghost.
Come into our lives.
Teach us how to keep our lives in your sight.
Let your spirit be completely in us.
In Jesus name, Amen

191

Forevermore

Forevermore: I will love you my Lord Jesus.

Forevermore: I will wait for you my Lord Jesus.

Forevermore: I will always count on you my Lord Jesus.

Forevermore: I will always need you my Lord Jesus.

Forevermore: I will give you my soul my Lord Jesus.

Forevermore: I will give you my heart my Lord Jesus.

Forevermore: I will give you my mind my Lord Jesus.

Forevermore: I will give you all praise my Lord Jesus.

Forevermore: I will give you all glory my Lord Jesus.

Forevermore: I will give my life for you my Lord Jesus.

Forevermore: You will always be my blessed Savior my Lord Jesus.

Forevermore: You will always be my joy my Lord Jesus.

Forevermore: You will always be everything my Lord Jesus.

Forevermore: You will always be my forevermore my Lord Jesus.
In Jesus name, Amen

192

Happiness

Our Lord Jesus Christ is our happiness.
He is the one that gives us the loved ones that make us smile.
In this life it is not enough to have the world and to be very unhappy.
In this life we must find what really makes us happy.
In this life I just want to be with my loved ones.
Just to see their faces, to here there voice every moment of the day.
Know their smiles have given me a lot of joy in my life.
I have loved all of them, since I laid my eyes upon them.
Because in their smile, is where I found the face of God smiling back at me everyday.
You are the song in the wind.
You are the echo that God sings in my heart.
My love for you is more than all the stars in the sky.
You are what God blessed me with to be happy.
That is why I love our Lord Jesus Christ.
Always close to us day and night.
I believe we made it this far because of the watchful eyes of our Lord Jesus Christ.
For there is no time in my life, I would want to live without our Father or our Lord Jesus Christ.

In this life we all have sinned.
Our Lord Jesus Christ has forgiven us every time.
He is our solder.
He is our captain.
He is what we breathe.
He is the leader of the band.
He is the light of the World.
He is our Glory.
That's why I love our Lord Jesus Christ.
With all my heart he gave me life and all that I love.
Jesus shall always be my first love.
My children shall always be my happiness.
They are a gift from God.
So, I will always pray and call on you God for everything I need.
It is a blessing to know that our Lord Jesus Christ will always be our light.
That he will always be the answer to our lives.
Always be that smile up on our faces.
Let it be with God where our happiness lies in our lives.
In Jesus name, Amen

193

My Everlasting Love

You are my life; you are my only true love. Lord you will always be my everlasting love.
It is a blessing to have God to be your everlasting love.

My everlasting love, melt me into your heart Lord.

My everlasting love, pull me into Thou soul Lord.

My everlasting love, surround me with your truth Lord.

My everlasting love unconditionally is forever in my life Lord.

My everlasting love, I will follow you step by step Lord.

My everlasting love, certainly I know you will always be by my side Lord.

My everlasting love is the power that gives me strength Lord.

My everlasting love, my soul seeks only you Lord.

My everlasting love, precious is the light you shine in me Lord.

My everlasting love, I sought you out in my soul and found you waiting for me in my heart Lord.

My everlasting love, my desire is to lie in your arms forever Lord,

My everlasting love, patiently I wait for your coming, forever I will love you Lord.
Forever in you will be my everlasting love Lord.
In Jesus name, Amen

194

Let heaven hear your praise

I fell down, did not know how to get up again.
You came alone picking up my life again.
I found God when things in my life seem to go wrong.
You turn my world around.
I was lost in myself.
You came to show me the right direction.

If you know God is good clap your hands and let heaven hear your praise,
If you know Jesus is the Son of God stomp your feet and let heaven hear your praise.
If you know the Holy Ghost is real wave your hands and let heaven hear your praise.
If you believe in the Father clap your hands and let heaven hear your praise.
If you believe in the Savior, stomp your feet and let heaven hear your praise.
If you believe in the Holy Ghost wave your hands and let heaven hear your praise.

I could not walk anymore.
You carried me until I was ready to walk on my own.
When thing around me were draining my life.
You poured out your strength in me.
When my feet step off the path you guided me back with your light.
If you believe in God, the Son and Holy Ghost clap your hands and let heaven hear your praise.
In Jesus name, Amen

195

Joy, Joy, Joy

Joy, Joy, Joy is my Lord.
So Kind,
So Sweet,
So Beautiful,
Joy, Joy, Joy in my heart,
In my Soul,
In my Life,
You are my Joy,
Lord Jesus Christ.

Joy, Joy, Joy is my Lord.
So Wonderful,
So Gracious,
So Sincere,
Joy, Joy, Joy in my heart,
In my Soul,
In my Life,
You are my Joy,
Lord Jesus Christ.

Joy, Joy, Joy is my Lord.
So Precious,
So Splendid,
So Loving,
Joy, Joy, Joy in my heart,
In my Soul,
In my Life,
You are my Joy,
Lord Jesus Christ.

Joy, Joy, Joy is my Lord.
So Blessed,
So Pure,
So Fresh,
Joy, Joy, Joy in my Heart,
In my Soul,
In my Life,
You are my Joy,
Lord Jesus Christ.

Joy, Joy, Joy is my Lord.
So Needed,
So Wanted,
So Holy,
Joy, Joy, Joy in my Heart,
In my Soul,
In my Life,
You are the Joy,
Lord Jesus Christ
Joy, Joy, Joy that is what you are, Lord Jesus Christ,
In Jesus name, Amen

196

Answer

Don't lose hope, when you can't figure it out.
Let God be your answer.
Don't give up on hope; don't do it on your own, but when it comes out wrong.
Let God be your answer.
Don't say that hope is gone; you might just break your own spirit.
Let God be your answer.

God I will not give up on you Jesus is our Savior.
I will hold hope deep in my heart, wrapped in my arms.
I will call on you when trouble comes.
God I will trust in you, Jesus is our Savior.
Because I won't give up on you, I will not let my faith fail me.
God through Jesus you are the answer.
I will always believe in you.

Hold your tongue when you don't know the answer.
You might just lead yourself down the wrong way.
Let God be your answer.
Keep your doubt to yourself; don't play like you know the answer.
Let God be your answer.
God maybe listening to how much faith you have.
Don't break His heart, have faith in the Lord.
Let God be your answer.
In Jesus name, Amen

197

Trust in the Lord

Give him all your dreams.
Give him all your wishes.
Give him all your hopes.
And let God go to work for you.
Let him bring your prayers to the light.
Don't be afraid to walk behind God.
Let him lead the way in your life.
Trust in the Lord.

Trust in the Lord; don't walk away from God.
Listen to what the Lord has to say.
Trust in the Lord, you don't want to miss him when he comes through.
What the word of the Lord can do for you.
Trust in the Lord.
You don't want to get lost in this world without the Lord watching over you.

Trust in the Lord, he will always be there.
Trust in the Lord, call on his name.
Trust in the lord, Jesus hears all prayers the first time.
Trust in the Lord.

Trust in the Lord, don't look away.
Keep your eyes on the Lord.
Trust in the Lord, you don't want to miss when he comes through.
In a dream I see the coming of the Lord on the wings of a dove with open arms.
Trust in the Lord, he is always there by your side.
His love dries your eyes when you cry.
He is the joy of God Our Lord,
Trust in the Lord.
In Jesus name, Amen

198

Without the blessing of God

I don't believe that my on strength can move me without the blessing of God.
I don't believe that I can do it on my own without the blessing of God.
I don't believe that tomorrow will come without the blessing of God.

I trust in your God.
You are my hero.
You are the glory that breathes in me.
My life is yours.
My soul is fed by you.
I hunger for your love.
I thirst for your word.
Too guide my way in your direction.
My heart sings hallelujah is your name.
I would not see the light without the blessing of God.
Peace to the Father, the Son and the Holy Ghost.

I give you all honor and praise.
I don't believe in anything in this world without the blessing of God.
I don't believe I woke up on my own without the blessing of God.
I don't believe that I would make it each day without the blessing of God.
Praise to the Father, the Son and the Holy Ghost.
In Jesus name Amen

199

I remember you prayed for me

I remember when I was a little child.
You kept me out of harm's way.
You blessed my days.
I remember you prayed for me.

I remember when I got older but still yet a child.
You kept me out of trouble.
You blessed my steps.
I remember you prayed for me.

I remember when I became a young adult.
You kept me out of the wrong crowd.
You blessed my mind.
I remember you prayed for me.

I remember when I became a little older.
You kept me in the right direction.
You blessed my path.
I remember you prayed for me.

I remember to thank you everyday.
As I grow old I remember to pray.
In my life I give you Praise.
Glorify your name.
You blessed me with your prayers.
I remember you Jesus, when you prayed for me.

Keep praying for me, all the time.
My Lord Jesus Christ, Amen.
In Jesus name, Amen

200

In Jesus name, thank you Father

I hope I will walk always in the glory of God the Father.
I thank you God for being by my side all the time.
In Jesus name, thank you Father.

I hope I will walk always in the mercy of God the Father.
I thank you God for being in my life all the time,
In Jesus name, thank you Father.

I hope I will walk always in the joy of God the Father.
I thank you God for being here in my heart all the time.
In Jesus name, thank you Father.

I hope I will walk always in the blessing of God the Father.
I thank you God for being here in my soul all the time.
In Jesus name, thank you Father.

I hope I will walk always in the guidance of God the Father.
I thank you God for being all my strength all the time.
In Jesus name, thank you Father.
In Jesus name, Amen

201

Always here by my side

You Lord are the peace always, every way in me.
You are my salvation, always here by my side.

You Lord are the joy always, every way in me.
You are my true love, always here by my side.

You Lord are the courage always, every way in me.
You are my truth, always here by my side.

You Lord are the glory always, every way in me.
You are my life, always here by my side.

You Lord are the mercy always, every way in me.
You are my trust, always here by my side.

You Lord, are the love always, every way in me.
You are my comfort, always here by my side.

You Lord are the grace always, every way in me.
You are my righteousness, always here by my side.

You Lord are the blessing always, every way in me.
You are my hope, always here by my side.

You Lord are the truth always, every way in me.
You are my gentle touch, always here by my side.

You Lord are the believer always, every way in me.
You are my soul, always here by my side.

You Lord are the thanksgiving always, every way in me.
You are my heart, always here by my side.

You Lord are the strength always, every way in me.
You are my light, always here by my side.

You Lord are the want always, every way in me.
You are my breath, always here by my side.
You are everything living in me.
In Jesus name, Amen

202

Only Jesus

There are times we don't understand.
Why things don't go like we plan.
We feel so lost in ourselves.
So sad when we don't know which way too go?
Oh, how we hope we could start the day all over again.
To change the way it ends, without tears my Lord.
Only Jesus can help us to understand.

Only Jesus can comfort you now.
Only Jesus can make you smile.
Only Jesus can change your day.
Only Jesus can dry your eyes.
Only Jesus can make you happy.
Only Jesus can make you glad.
Only Jesus can heal your soul.
Only Jesus can put joy in a broken heart.
Only Jesus can take away the pain.
Only Jesus can turn fear into courage.

We may not understand.
Why this must be.
Comfort us in our need.
Be with us, through it all. No matter how we cry.
Pray for us in our time of needs.
Only Jesus can make away in our lives.
In your name Lord Jesus,
Amen.

203

Lean on the Lord Jesus

Things don't always go right in our life.
We look for understanding that can't be found.
We must lean on the Lord Jesus Christ.

We put a smile on our face.
Trying hard to hide the way we really feel.
But inside sadness grows
We must lean on the Lord Jesus Christ.

There are so many questions.
We try hard to find the answers.
But all the answers are in God's hands.
We must lean on the Lord Jesus Christ.

No matter how hard things get.
We must find it in our hearts to trust in God's will.
Lord let your thunder stand at our side.
Lord let the rain wash us clean.
Lord let your lighting be the light that guides our way home.
Let us see your Glory walk cross the clouds.
With open arms too comfort us in our pain.
Our tear seems to dry before falling from our eyes.
The softness of His hand came from nowhere and gave joy.
But we cry because Jesus' love flows like a river inside.
We must lean on the Lord Jesus Christ.
In Jesus name, Amen

204

Spirit

Oh, how Jesus loves us with His whole heart.
Oh, how Sincere your love has grown in our hearts.

Oh, how Jesus loves us with His whole heart.
Oh, how perfect your love has grown in our hearts.

Oh, how Jesus loves us with His whole heart.
Oh, how incredible your love has grown in our hearts.

Oh, how Jesus loves us with His whole heart.
Oh, how sweet your love has grown in our hearts.

Oh, how Jesus loves us with His whole heart.
Oh, how beautiful your love has grown in our hearts.

Oh, how Jesus loves us with His whole heart.
Oh, how true your love has grown in our hearts.

Oh, how Jesus loves us with His whole heart.
Oh, how gentle your love has grown in our hearts.

Oh, how our Spirit love you Jesus all the time with our whole heart.
I love my lord Jesus with every breath.
He is my life.
He is the spirit that travels through me every moment in my life.
In Jesus name, Amen

205

The light

God is the light that guides you.
Through all your troubles that come into your life.
Through all your broken hearts, that pain that walks all over your heart.
God is the light that dries your eyes

Jesus is the light that grows within you.
Through all your hardships, your burden that set upon your shoulders.
Through all your fears that has scared you in life.
Through all the days that has gone wrong.
Jesus is the light that shines in you.

The Holy Ghost is the light that set round you.
Through all the times you suffered in your life.
Through all your problems that took too much from your life.
Through all the nights you feel lost.
The Holy Ghost is the light that finds your way home.

They are your courage, your strong hold, your foundation and strength.
Their light never burn out. They are the light that will always light your way through life.
Our Father, the Son and the Holy Ghost
They are the light in you.
In Jesus name, Amen

206

Songs of my Heart

God you are the song that sing over and over I love you in my heart.
Lord your voice echo with pure love into my soul.
Each day that pass I find myself loving you more.
I feel my heart dancing in your love.
I feel the music that sings your love to my soul.
Lord you are the songs of my heart lyrics of love.

God you are the melody that hums softly in and out my heart. As I feel your love running in my heart.
You are the hem that humbles your love in my soul.
Each day that pass I find His love has deepened itself in my soul even more.
I feel my love stirring up itself in your heart.
I feel so weak letting your love take over my soul.
Lord you are the songs of my heart lyrics of love

God you are the sweet sound of joy with love that goes around in my heart.
You are the tears of peacefulness that cries a tone of love in my soul.
Each day that passes His love grips my heart and my soul fall forever into your hands.
I feel my heart breathing in your love.
I feel your gentle love moving always in my soul.
Lord you are the songs of my heart lyrics of love.
In Jesus name, Amen

207

Amen

His breath wakes up my life every moment.
Amen, Amen, Amen

Your beautiful heart died upon a cross.
Amen, Amen, Amen

Every face you put before me I see you looking back at me
Amen, Amen, Amen

Hearing the voices of my loved ones once again is a gift from you.
Amen, Amen, Amen

His joy is what he gives us every day.
Amen, Amen, Amen

A love that gave up His only begotten joy nailed to the cross.
Amen, Amen, Amen

You are the hugs and kisses from all that I love.
Amen, Amen, Amen

Glory lesson to the prayers of my soul calling for forgiveness of it sins.
Amen, Amen, Amen

Lord you are an every day blessing to have in my life, thank you.
Amen, Amen, Amen

Each smile I see I feel your presence smiling back at me so beautiful.
Amen, Amen, Amen

My devotion gives you my life, my soul, my love and Father you are every breath of my heart.
Amen, Amen, Amen
In Jesus Name Amen

208

Let the Hand of God the Father

Let the hand of God the Father remove the evil people out of our lives.
Clean up their mess and sweep them out the door.
Close it behind them and let them not come into our lives anymore.
In the name of our Lord and Savior, Jesus Christ Amen.

Be there always Lord

I pray that God the Father bless The Songs of my Heart.
I pray that I will always love God, His children and myself.
Believe in Him, Have faith in Him and always trust Him with everything.
He is the hope we need.
He is the gentle voice that guides us.
Be there always Lord to help us in our lives.
Your company is more than a blessing.
A gift from you is when you never leave our side.
You are the blessing and joy we need in our lives always and forever.
Always hear the prayers of my heart my Father.
Answer them with your merciful loving kind heart.
Be there always Lord to hear us when we call.
In the name of our Lord and Savior, Jesus Christ Amen.

These songs set in my soul forever, God you're the lyrics of love that has been singing forever in my heart.
Has become songs of poems dedicated to you Father, Son and the Holy Ghost.
You are the songs of my heart, lyrics of love God, Father in Jesus name Amen.

May God's love, hope, joy and his blessing follow us everywhere in our life?
Always pray to find yourself walking in peace with God, Father in Jesus name Amen.

Four prayers to help us alone our journey 5

Songs of my Heart 1 to 207 and Prayer of my Heart 5
By Beshera L Crowley
Pages 1 to 213
209

God bless every step and everyday you gives us, Father in Jesus name Amen:

Songs of my Heart Index:
Pages 1 to 214